Arts-Based Research Methods in Writing Studies

As the arts become an increasingly popular pedagogical tool in writing studies, *Arts-Based Research Methods in Writing Studies* offers scholars and educators in the field ways to leverage the arts for their own scholarship through the practice of arts-based research (ABR).

Tailored to the needs of writing studies scholars, this concise guide presents ways of exploring and addressing unresolved research questions from the past as well as new, pressing questions that are emerging in light of increasingly fraught and complicated current contexts. It explores motives and methods for taking up ABR, sheds light on the processes of representing research and the ethical imperative of methodological disclosure, and looks critically at the complexities of fully realizing ABR in writing studies while offering some pedagogical applications. Connecting theory to practice, this book also performs ABR through a co-created mixed-media text about the everyday and extraordinary stories woven into the fabric of new American artists' composing processes.

Arts-Based Research Methods in Writing Studies lends itself to insight that is at once personal for writing studies researchers, useful for research communities, and a catalyst for social change beyond institutional walls; as such, it will be an important resource for scholars, educators, and graduate students in writing studies and those interested in multimodal, multilingual, and translingual learning; equitable pedagogies and administrative practices; online writing instruction; transnational literacies; research methods; community-based research; and disability studies in composition.

Kate Hanzalik is an assistant teaching professor in the Department of Writing Studies, Rhetoric, and Composition at Syracuse University. She co-edited *Exquisite Corpse: Studio Art-Based Writing in the Academy* with Natalie Virgintino, and holds a Ph.D. in Rhetorics, Communication, and Information Design from Clemson University, an M.F.A. in Writing from The Savannah College of Art and Design, and an M.A. in Liberal Studies from Dartmouth College.

Routledge Research in Writing Studies

Writing Center Talk Over Time
A Mixed-Method Study
Jo Mackiewicz

Writing Support for International Graduate Students
Enhancing Transition and Success
Shyam Sharma

Rhetorical Strategies for Professional Development
Investment Mentoring in Classrooms and Workplaces
Elizabeth J. Keller

Digital Reading and Writing in Composition Studies
Edited by Mary R. Lamb and Jennifer Parrott

Writing Democracy
Taking the Political Turn In and Beyond The Trump Era
Edited by Shannon Carter, Deborah Mutnick, Stephen Parks, and Jessica Pauszek

Writing Centers at the Center of Change
Edited by Joe Essid & Brian McTague

Teaching Writing, Rhetoric, and Reason at the Globalizing University
Robert Samuels

Arts-Based Research Methods in Writing Studies
A Primer
Kate Hanzalik

Arts-Based Research Methods in Writing Studies

A Primer

Kate Hanzalik

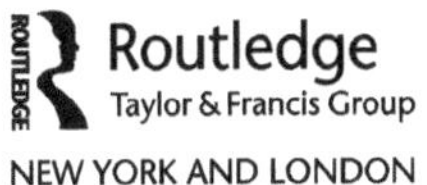

NEW YORK AND LONDON

First published 2021
by Routledge
52 Vanderbilt Avenue, New York, NY 10017

and by Routledge
2 Park Square, Milton Park, Abingdon, Oxon, OX14 4RN

Routledge is an imprint of the Taylor & Francis Group, an informa business

Library of Congress Cataloging-in-Publication Data
A catalog record for this book has been requested

ISBN: 978-0-367-56706-4 (hbk)
ISBN: 978-0-367-56814-6 (pbk)
ISBN: 978-1-003-09944-4 (ebk)

Typeset in Times New Roman
by Apex CoVantage, LLC

For Jodi Corley, In lieu of doxa

Contents

Figures

Tables

Abbreviations

ABR	Arts-Based Research
MD	Methodological Disclosure
PaR	Practice as Research
RC	Research Creation
TAP	Think-aloud Protocol
WS	Writing Studies

Acknowledgments

I wish to acknowledge many people and organizations who have helped bring this project to life, starting with my colleagues, friends, and former professors who offered their insight on this project. Thank you to Mary Doll, Amy Condon, Mark Bousquet, Alan Lelchuk, Fethi Keles, Catherine Gerard, Beth Hewett, and Janet Zepernick. Many thanks to Nathalie Virgintino, Brian Gaines, and Vittoria Rubino, whose exciting scholarship and innovative ideas stand out among those advocating for the arts in writing studies. To the faculty in the Rhetorics, Communication, and Information Design doctoral program at Clemson University—without Victor Vitanza, Cynthia Haynes, Dave Blakesley, Steve Katz, and Jan Holmevik, I would not have taken the risks I have taken with my scholarship. Your ingenuity, innovation, open-mindedness, and support have made all the difference. Thank you to my editor, Suzanne Richardson, whose interest in this project made it possible, and to Sukriti Pandey, Grant Schatzman, and Aruna Rajendran, who helped bring the manuscript to life. A special thanks goes to the Maxwell School of Citizenship and the Program for the Advancement of Research on Conflict and Collaboration at Syracuse University. To Kristi Johnson, thank you for your administrative support. To Cyprien Mihigo, Charlotte Mihigo, Gayle Riina, the New American Forum, and the Congolese Women's Empowerment Sewing Group, thank you for sharing your perspectives on the complex, diverse experiences of new Americans in Syracuse, New York. I am especially grateful for my family, Albert, Barbara, Scott, Helena, Caleb, Gabriella, and the Pennisi family. I will forever cherish our memories and time spent in the Sanctuary City. Most of all, I want to thank Mmalanibwa LoseLose and Nada Odeh for sharing your stories and composing practices, advancing disciplinary knowledge, community-engaged scholarship, and the understanding that artists can make the world a better place.

Introduction

The Allure of Arts-Based Research

Arts-based research (ABR) is a process by which scholars and/or their research participants engage the arts to shed light on a topic, problem, or question (McNiff, 2008). ABR can be used at any stage or moment of the research process; its goal is to use artistic ways of knowing to produce new knowledge. Because of its privileging of the personal and subjective and its origins in the creative and imaginative arts, ABR has faced challenges and criticism, as this book will go on to discuss. Yet, new understandings and meanings are made possible with and through an arts-based research process.

As a research method, ABR is designed to explore the subjective spaces of feelings, ambiguity, and perspective to reveal what other forms of research overlook. For the field of writing studies (WS), this might seem like familiar territory as WS has close family relationships to literature and creative writing, where the role of the arts in exploring, revealing, and expressing the human condition is understood to be an essential foundation of our discipline. That is true. But ABR, unlike other forms of research in our disciplinary toolkit, is characterized by the use of creative art forms not just to make knowledge but to make knowledge about knowledge, using the visual, literary, and performing arts to study the works, processes, and situations that are the subject matter of our discipline. In this way, art itself becomes the expression and performance of research rather than solely the object of research.

The term "art" is often recast in the WS lexicon as a type of composition: a work of art can be understood as a "multimodal" composition (Palmeri, 2012); art has been described as "multiwriting" and as an "alternative composition" (Davis and Shadle, 2007), a type of literacy or "multiple literacies," "experimental" composition (Bishop, 1997). Art, as part of "other creative genres" (Conference), has been described by scholars in the field as "non-alphetic ways of knowing," "other ways of knowing" (Dunn, 2001), and "non-linguistic signifying system[s]" (Shipka, 2011). Some have criticized the arts, noting that "The picture is easier than the essay. . . non-verbal assignments do not do the 'serious work' of an English class, which is to teach writing" (Pierpoint, 1996, as cited in Dunn, 2001, p. 150). Some have made a mockery of the arts, proclaiming, for example, that they would perform a dance for their committee instead of present a conventional dissertation (see Soper, 2000, as cited in Dunn, 2011). Yet performative forms of research are happening in WS: for example, autoethnography (Canagarajah, 2012), institutional ethnography (LaFrance, 2019), counterstory (Martinez, 2014, 2016, 2019, 2020), and a rapp album and mix-tap/e/ssay (Carson, 2017, 2020a). Two collections, *Exquisite Corpse: Studio Art-Based Writing in the Academy* (Hanzalik and Virgintino, 2019) and *Writing in and about the Visual and Performing Arts* (Corbett et al., 2019), both reflect on and perform art in WS research and pedagogy.

ABR research designs can be systematic or wildly recursive. They can take many different directions, and art-making can take place at different stages or in all stages of a project. Oftentimes, ABR does not have a predetermined research design but emerges extemporaneously. Art-making as scholarship is situated in a scholarly setting, and those who engage in it are at once scholars and artists. Yet investigative art made outside institutional walls can also be considered ABR, which means there are many possibilities for transdisciplinary collaboration. ABR presents new ways of exploring and addressing unresolved research questions from the past as well as new, pressing questions that are emerging in light of increasingly fraught and complicated current contexts.

Although new to WS, ABR and its analogues, such as a/r/tography, practice as research (PaR), and research creation (RC), have a history in art therapy (Allen, 1995; McNiff, 1998, 2013), art education (Irwin and De Cosson, 2004; Loveless, 2019; Nelson, 2013; Prior and McNiff, 2018; Rolling, 2013; Sullivan, 2005, 2010), education (Barone and Eisner, 1997, 2011; Cahnmann-Taylor and Siegesmund, 2018), disabilities studies (Allen, 2019), hip-hop studies (Carson, 2017, 2020a), and in the social sciences more broadly (Finley, 2008, 2017; Lawrence-Lightfoot and Davis, 1997; Lawrence-Lightfoot, n.d.; Leavy, 2009, 2017, 2019; Lenette, 2019; O'Neill, 2008). Scholars in these disciplines are drawn to ABR because it adds evocative and expressive potential to the analytical options present in other research forms and creates opportunities to engage audiences in an immediate way, to reach broader audiences who might be compelled to take action, and to engage in forms of personal inquiry that might be therapeutic for both the researcher and research participants. ABR also creates opportunities to challenge and present alternatives to dominant research paradigms and practices, an important goal at a time when disciplines in the social sciences and humanities, including WS, are beginning to recognize the extent to which their research practices have tended to promote the persistence of entrenched views that are resistant to voices from outside the privileged (and typically white-dominant) mainstream.

In WS, Vittoria Rubino (2019a) was the first scholar to see that ABR could be incorporated into the discipline's methods. In "The Artistry of Composition: Towards an Arts-Based Pedagogy for First-Year Composition," she traced the history of ABR from the psychologist Rudolph Arnheim in the mid-twentieth century to contemporary arts educators, social scientists, and art therapists and argues that

> new research methodologies are emerging, and I would suggest research done in the arts can be valuable to the first-year composition classroom because of its transdisciplinary nature. Most interestingly in arts-based research, for example, students may use the process of drawing to learn more about a specific aspect of drawing, to draw on their artistic intelligence in relation to a topic, or to reflect on their own experiences although arts-based research includes everything from painting to creative writing to dance and beyond.
>
> (2019, p. 90)

Following Rubino and other scholars across a range of disciplines who have taken part in the evolving ABR conversation, this book seeks to extend the focus from ABR's potential as pedagogy to how ABR fits into disciplinary research expectations, styles, and standards for publication. Additionally, this book focuses on how WS scholars can use ABR to serve communities and cultures outside the university through the arts, while also incorporating ABR into their research about topics specific to WS. If, as Rubino says, "history is still being written on arts-based research" (2019a, p. 6), then this book strives to contribute to that history.

Research in WS, broadly speaking, focuses on learning, teaching, and communication. The questions, concerns, and problems that researchers take up are multiple and continually evolving as the political, social, technological, and institutional contexts change. The present turn to ABR in WS is timely because the issues that have become, or continue to be, especially salient in the second decade of this new century are ones that require new ways of seeing—something for which ABR is distinctly well suited. Questions such as the nature of equitable pedagogies (Inoue, 2015; Lerner, 2019; Martinez, 2014, 2016, 2019, 2020; Young and Martinez, 2011) and multimodal, multilingual, and translingual learning (Bazerman et al., 2019; Canagarajah, 2012; Frost et al., 2020; Khadka, 2019; Palmeri, 2012) and the practical and sociopolitical implications of online writing instruction and remote or distance learning (Borgman et al., 2020; Hewett et al., 2015; Monske and Blair, 2017) are profoundly interwoven with both global and local issues that have been elevated in researchers' and educators' minds through a global pandemic, recent protests, and subsequent societal and cultural shifts. The year 2020 in particular has revealed that business as usual is not working.

The intentions and capacities of ABR, as described by education researcher Susan Finley, are closely aligned with WS work:

> By its integration of multiple methodologies used in the arts with the postmodern ethics of participative, action-oriented, and politically situated perspectives for human social inquiry, arts-based inquiry has the potential to facilitate critical race, indigenous, queer, feminist, and border theories and research methodologies. As a form of performance pedagogy, arts-based inquiry can be used to advance a subversive political agenda that addresses issues of social inequity. Such work exposes oppression, targets sites of resistance, and outlines possibilities for transformative praxis. From this perspective, arts-based inquiry can explore multiple, new, and diverse ways of understanding and living in the world.
>
> (2008, p. 72)

ABR offers researchers creative ways to get at WS problems and may lead to new research approaches and new answers, from which may come new considerations of human-focused writing instruction. ABR can be used to address sensitive issues with creative approaches that enable diversity of voices and means to express what previously has been difficult to express, using various combinations and permutations of alphabetic and mixed-media research. Used well, ABR can address unresolved problems in new ways and to new ends. It can be used in conjunction with and to enhance traditional research methods to, for example, offer new options for documenting the composing process or relating to research participants. ABR can extend the purposes of WS research in service of other disciplines as well as of broader communities and marginalized people beyond the academy. Finally, but not least, ABR can provide scholars with new opportunities for self-discovery and expression through the research process.

As I will go on to discuss, ABR deserves a rightful place in the conversation about research in WS, most notably, although not exclusively, because it responds to pressing issues in WS and meets current research needs. ABR should be situated within WS's ongoing dialogue about the quantitative and qualitative paradigms, mainly because it can advance that dialogue as well as the arts-based writing movement trending in so many disciplines. ABR and its analogues—arts-based educational research, a/r/tography, PaR, and RC—have begun to take up these approaches. Ultimately these fields reflect what WS research can continue to do—produce new and exciting knowledge that is changing the way scholars and artists are engaging with and changing the world.

Overview of the Chapters

The first chapter sheds light on WS's current conversations, needs and interests for research, and how the field has a history of incorporating the arts into its research. Drawing distinctions between the qualitative, quantitative, and arts-based paradigms, the chapter also shows how ABR can help to address specific questions or realize new ones that are worth exploring. The structure of the remainder of the book suggests that ABR is a standardized procedure. The second chapter, "Motives and Methods for Arts-Based Research," provides readers with a starting point for designing an ABR project. I offer some reasons to take up ABR and some specific methodologies, methods, and genres that might be amenable to various research purposes. In the third chapter, "Representing Research in Art Form," I show and tell how sharing research in art form is an emotional and intellectually rigorous process and product, one that can, although does not have to, demonstrate some degree of technical mastery. The fourth chapter, "Methodological Disclosure in Arts-Based Research," draws from scholars in different disciplines to explain why and how ABR researchers should reflect on their research projects. The final chapter, "A Promising Future for Arts-Based Research Methods in Writing Studies," offers some pedagogical applications and leaves readers with salient questions with which researchers must grapple if they are to take up ABR. Throughout the chapters, I discuss, perform, and reflect on my ABR project, drawing connections between the theories I present with my experiences engaging in ABR.

Despite what the linear arrangement of this book suggests, ABR is highly recursive. Research problems are replaced with motives, which can be discovered through a method or in a form of representation. The site where the research is shared might become a new site of research. The methodology might change the researcher's motive or incite several additional motives, resulting in a revision to the methodology, a process that might then serve as data for an ongoing ABR methodology rather than one that is ad hoc. Finally, answers to research questions are often ambiguous affectations. Some scholars argue that ABR can be systematic—they can begin with a research question that can lead to a generalizable, useful conclusion—yet getting to the end result is not so clear cut. My own research studying dozens of examples of ABR projects, reading numerous books and articles about theories and methods, and designing my own ABR project leads me to agree with Sullivan, who argues that

> Artistic practice can be seen to comprise a critical coalition of practices that involve an ongoing dialogue within and across and between and around the artist, artwork, and context, where each has a role to play in the pursuit of understanding.
>
> (2010, p. 199)

At the heart of that statement is a provocation, one that challenges WS to accept art on its own terms.

Arts-Based Research Methods in Writing Studies is merely an etching of ABR for WS scholars. I provide guidance on how ABR might inform, enhance, and advance WS research interests. It is impossible to give readers a comprehensive set of ideas and recommendations for all the diverse and intricate range of topics the field takes up—particularly because ABR is so recursive and only now emerging in WS and because ingenuity is among the defining characteristics of the remarkable scholars and educators in WS. It is my sincere hope that this book sufficiently justifies art as a valuable way of knowing and a credible means of creating knowledge.

References

Allen, A. (2019). Intersecting arts based research and disability studies: Suggestions for art education curriculum centered on disability identity development. *Journal of Curriculum Theorizing, 34*(1), 72–82.

Allen, P. B. (1995). *Art is a way of knowing: A guide to self-knowledge and spiritual fulfillment through creativity*. Boulder: Shambhala Publications.

Barone, T., & Eisner, E. W. (1997). Arts-based educational research. In R. M Jaeger (Ed.), *Complementary methods for research in education* (pp. 73–99). Washington, DC: American Educational Research Association.

———. (2011). *Arts based research*. Los Angeles, CA: Sage Publications.

Bazerman, C., González Pinzón, B. Y., Russell, D., Rogers, P., Bernardo Peña, L., Narváez, E., Carlino, P., & Castelló, M., & Tapia-Ladino, M. (Eds.). (2019). *Conocer la Escritura: Investigación Más Allá de las Frontera [Knowing writing: Writing research across borders]*. International Exchanges on the Study of Writing. Bogota, DC and Fort Collins, CO: Editorial Pontificia Universidad Javeriana and The WAC Clearinghouse. https://wac.colostate.edu/books/wrab2017/.

Bishop, W. (Ed.). (1997). *Elements of alternate style: Essays on writing and revision*. Portsmouth, NH: Heinemann Educational Publishers.

Borgman, J., & McArdle, C. (2020). *Personal, accessible, responsive, strategic: Resources and strategies for online writing instructors*. Boulder, CO: University of Colorado Press.

Cahnmann-Taylor, M., & Siegesmund, R. (Eds.). (2018). *Arts-based research in education: Foundations for practice*. Abingdon, UK: Routledge.

Canagarajah, A. S. (2012). *Translingual practice: Global Englishes and cosmopolitan relations*. Milton Park, Abingdon, Oxon, and New York: Routledge. doi: 10.4324/9780203073889.

Conference on College Composition and Communication. (2018). *Scholarship in rhetoric, writing, and composition: Guidelines for faculty, deans, and chairs* (2nd ed.). https://cccc.ncte.org/cccc/resources/positions/scholarshipincomp.

Corbett, S. J., LeMesurier, J. L., Decker, T. E., & Cooper, B. (Eds.). (2019). *Writing in and about the performing and visual arts: Creating, performing, and teaching.*

Across the Disciplines Books. Fort Collins, CO: The WAC Clearinghouse and University Press of Colorado.

Davis, R. L., & Shadle, M. F. (2007). *Teaching multiwriting: Researching and composing with multiple genres, media, disciplines, and cultures*. Carbondale, IL: Southern Illinois University Press.

Dunn, P. (2001). *Talking, sketching, moving: Multiple literacies in the teaching of writing*. Portsmouth, NH: Boynton/Cook – Heinemann.

Finley, S. (2008). Arts-based research. In J. G. Knowles & A. L. Cole (Eds.), *Handbook of the arts in qualitative research: Perspectives, methodologies, examples, and issues* (pp. 72–82). Thousand Oaks, CA: Sage Publications. doi: 10.4135/9781452226545.n6.

———. (2017). Critical arts-based inquiry: Performances of resistance politics. In N. K. Denzin & Y. S. Lincoln (Eds.), *The SAGE handbook of qualitative research* (pp. 561–575). Thousand Oaks, CA: Sage Publications.

Hanzalik, K., & Virgintino, N. (2019). Social justice in (and beyond) the studio art-based classroom: Improvisation and play as responses to economic inequality. In K. Hanzalik & N. Virgintino (Eds.), *Exquisite corpse: Studio art-based writing in the academy* (pp. 173–196). Anderson, SC: Parlor Press.

Hewett, B. L., DePew, K. E., Guler, E., & Warner, R. Z. (Eds.). (2015). *Foundational practices of online writing instruction*. Anderson, SC: Parlor Press.

Inoue, A. B. (2015). *Antiracist writing assessment ecologies: Teaching and assessing writing for a socially just future*. Anderson, SC: Parlor Press.

Irwin, R. L., & De Cosson, A. (Eds.). (2004). *A/r/tography: Rendering self through arts-based living inquiry*. Vancouver, CA: Pacific Educational Press.

LaFrance, M. (2019). *Institutional ethnography: A theory of practice for writing studies researchers*. Logan, UT: Utah State University Press.

Lawrence-Lightfoot, S. (n.d.). *Sara Lawrence-Lightfoot*. Retrieved from Saralawrence lightfoot.com.

Lawrence-Lightfoot, S., & Davis, J. H. (1997). *The art and science of portraiture*. San Francisco, CA: Jossey-Bass.

Leavy, P. (Ed.). (2009). *Method meets art: Arts-based research practice*. New York, NY: Guilford Press.

———. (2017). *Handbook of arts-based research*. New York, NY: Guilford Press.

———. (2019). *Spark*. New York, NY: The Guilford Press.

Lenette, C. (2019). *Arts-based methods in refugee research: Creating sanctuary*. Singapore: Springer.

Lerner, N. (2019). *Reformers, teachers, writers; Curricular and pedagogical inquiries*. Logan, UT: Utah State University Press.

Loveless, N. (2019). *How to make art at the end of the world: A manifesto for research-creation*. Durham, NC: Duke University Press.

Martinez, A. Y. (2014). A plea for critical race theory counterstory: Stock story versus counterstory dialogues concerning alejandra's "fit" in the academy. *Composition Studies*, *42*(2), 33–55.

———. (2016). Alejandra writes a book: A critical race counterstory about writing, identity, and being Chicanx in the academy. *Praxis: A Writing Center Journal*, *14*(1), 56–61.

———. (2019). Core-coursing counterstory: On master narrative histories of rhetorical studies curricula. *Rhetoric Review, 38*(4), 402–416. doi: 10.1080/07350198.2019.1655305.

———. (2020). *Counterstory: The rhetoric and writing of critical race theory*. Champaign, IL: Conference on College Composition and Communication, Studies in Writing and Rhetoric.

McNiff, S. (1998). *Art-based research*. Philadelphia, PA: Jessica Kingsley Publishers.

———. (2008). Art-based research. In J. G. Knowles & A. L. Cole (Eds.), *Handbook of the arts in qualitative research: Perspectives, methodologies, examples, and issues* (pp. 29–40). Los Angeles, CA: Sage Publications.

———. (2013). *Art as research: Opportunities and challenges*. Bristol, UK: Intellect Ltd.

Monske, E., & Blair, K. (Eds.). (2017). *Handbook of research on writing and composing in the age of MOOCs*. Hershey, PA: IGI Global.

Nelson, R. (2013). *Practice as research in the arts: Principles, protocols, pedagogies, resistances*. New York, NY: Palgrave MacMmllan.

O'Neill, M. (2008). Transnational refugees: The transformative role of art? *Forum: Qualitative Social Research, 9*(2), 59.

Palmeri, J. (2012). *Remixing composition: A history of multimodal writing pedagogy*. Carbondale, IL: Southern Illinois University Press.

Pierpoint, A. (1996). Letter to the editor. *English Journal, 85*(2), 11–12.

Prior, R. W., & McNiff, S. (2018). *Using art as research in learning and teaching: Multidisciplinary approaches across the arts*. Chicago, IL and Bristol, UK: Intellect Ltd.

Rolling, J. H. (2013). *Arts-based research*. New York, NY: Peter Lang Publishing.

Rubino, V. S. (2019a). *The artistry of composition: Towards an arts-based pedagogy for first-year composition*. A dissertation for St. John's University, New York.

Shipka, J. (2011). *Toward a composition made whole*. Pittsburgh, PA: University of Pittsburgh Press.

Soper, K. (2000, July 7). Things you shouldn't say at your dissertation defense. *The Chronicle of Higher Education*, B11.

Sullivan, G. (2005). *Art practice as research: Inquiry in visual arts*. Thousand Oaks, CA: Sage Publications.

———. (2010). *Art practice as research: Inquiry in visual arts*. Thousand Oaks, CA: Sage Publications.

Young, V. A., & Martinez, A. Y. (Eds.). (2011). *Code-meshing as world English: Pedagogy, policy, performance*. Urbana, IL: National Council of Teachers of English.

1 Writing Studies Research and the Place of the Arts

In this book, when I use the term writing studies (WS), I am also referring to rhetoric and composition. I do not mean to suggest that the terms can be conflated, but they are interrelated and often grouped together in conversations about research. The Conference on College Composition and Communication (CCCC) position statement, "Scholarship in Rhetoric, Writing, and Composition" (2018), offers a useful description of the domain of WS research:

> The work of scholars in the field is described by various interrelated terms, rhetoric, writing, and composition the most prominent. The interdisciplinary nature of this scholarship may also include or draw from scholarship institutional and administrative institutional and administrative practices; literacy studies; the scholarship of teaching and learning; communication; print and digital media; technical communication; second language studies/English as a second language; linguistics, and critical and cultural studies, among many others.

Understanding how knowledge is produced about/in the discipline can elucidate the exigences, relevance, and possibilities for ABR and vice versa. The literature illustrates that WS research generally focuses on "the practical, theoretical and ethical problems involved in any study of writing, whether in traditional or emerging subdisciplines" (Sheridan and Nickoson, 2012, p. 4). Books about research methods commonly critically assess a diverse range of methodologies and methods, with the shared purpose of envisioning new ideas for research and advancing the ways research is taken up (see Banks et al., 2019; Bazerman et al., 2012; Massey and Gebhard, 2011; Schell and Rawson, 2010; Sheridan and Nickoson, 2012). Readers can get a sense of the range of the field's research interests and approaches from five recent collections: *Writing Studies Research in Practice* (Sheridan and Nickoson, 2012), *The Changing Knowledge in Composition* (Massey and Gebhardt, 2011), *International Advances in Writing Research* (Bazerman et al., 2012), *Re/Orienting Writing Studies* (Banks et al., 2019), and *Rhetorica in Motion* (Schell and Rawson, 2010).

The field seeks to innovate where and how research is done. For example, Sheridan and Nickoson's (2012) collection of research reflections focus on "reimagining traditional research practices", such as ethnography (Sheridan and Nickoson, 2012, p. 12), narrative (Journet, 2012), and historical research (Rohan, 2012), "revisioning research in composition" (Sheridan and Nickoson, 2012, p. 99), such as ways to study and problematize discriminatory research practices about multilingual writers (Canagarajah, 2012) and assessment (Inoue, 2012, 2015), and "reconceptualizing methodologies and sites of inquiry" (Sheridan and Nickoson, 2012, p. 183), including an emphasis on sites such as the Internet (McKee and Porter, 2012), community-based research (Grabill, 2012), and international writing research (Lunsford, 2012). Massey and Gephardt's (2011) volume *The Changing of Knowledge in Composition* reflects on and advances the influential book *The Making of Knowledge in Composition* by Steven North, particularly as it relates to such topics as the identity and disciplinary status of writing and undergraduate and graduate education research methodologies. Schell and Rawson's (2010) volume responds to pressing questions about feminist research methods, such as "What are the key principles of feminist research?" (p. 7), "How can feminist research come to terms with the complexity of gender and other categories of social difference and lived experience?" (p. 7), and "What counts as evidence in feminist research and in feminist rhetoric in particular?" (p. 7). Contributors to Banks et al. (2019) discuss research from a queer perspective by reconsidering data-collection methods, making the case for the importance of failure and ambivalence in research, and rethinking empirical research, to name a few.

WS researchers are reworking old methods and inventing new ones to create their own "homegrown" mixed-method, project-specific approaches (Haas et al., 2012, p. 51) as well as developing collaborative, community-based approaches to understanding literacy practices, such as life-history (Selfe and Hawisher, 2012). They are also looking for ways that research can be shared with a broader audience and can be enhanced with technology (Sheridan and Nickoson, 2012). They seek opportunities for collaborative research involving students and teachers (Nickoson, 2012), more participatory, egalitarian approaches to research (Selfe and Hawisher, 2012), and more reflective writing about how researchers' identities shape their methodologies (Villanueva, 2011). As times change and new topics arise, scholars have expressed several concerns about the goals for research. This includes continued commitment to social justice (Poe et al., 2018) and more community-based research projects (Grabill, 2012). WS seeks methods that are adapted for disciplinary needs (Sheridan and Nickoson, 2012). While the aforementioned books and topics are in no way representative of all research and specialized topics in WS books, they do provide us with the kinds of questions, problems, and goals that researchers might want to approach in ways that are arts-based.

ABR can be taken up in many ways. For example, experiences, tensions, and stories are always woven into art, so collaborating with artists or arts organizations (Lenette, 2019) to create works that simultaneously illustrate and investigate research topics in WS can be generative. A researcher might collaborate with a photographer, or use photography to understand and convey community-based literacy practices to a broader audience while acknowledging the subjectivity of the researcher. Photographs can be taken in a number of ways depending on the researcher's purpose. They can be taken by the researcher themselves, by students as researchers, and/or by the research participants as researchers (Lenette, 2019). Analyzing data might involve everyone working together to identify patterns and meaning. The end product of the research could be a photography exhibit, held at a local or university art gallery, where a broader audience can learn about community-based literacy practices while providing a forum for dialogue that addresses the perspectives and stories present in the photographs. Writing would have its place in a curated exhibit. For example, an artist's statement can explain the project and discuss how specific techniques led to specific perspectives through which the research participants and community-based literacy practices are understood and felt. The possibilities for ABR projects in WS are as endless as the imaginations of the researchers themselves.

ABR lends itself to more flexibility when exploring any number of questions, topics, or problems because it disrupts conventional research standards (Barone and Eisner, 1997; McNiff, 2008; Leavy, 2009; Sullivan, 2005, 2010). Empirical standards, trusted by many in WS, include reliability (when the method can be repeated and lead to the same result), validity (when a research method tests what it is intended to test), generalizability (the applicability or usefulness of the research finding), and replicability (the method can be repeated). In ABR, high validity is a method that has affected the audience, taught them something new, and changed their values (Barone and Eisner, 1997). Validity is not a crucial standard, however, because many researchers do not gauge the reaction of their audience or factor that into their research design. Generalizability is not the standard of ABR per se, although researchers do consider high-quality ABR projects applicable (McNiff, 1998, 2013; Sullivan, 2005, 2010; Barone and Eisner, 2012). Credibility is one standard of ABR research, which strives for the audience's attunement to and belief in the artistic expression (Barone and Eisner, 2012). Good empirical research is rigorous and leads to a thesis;

arts-based research is good when it is vigorous (Faulkner, 2016) and conveys an exegesis instead of a thesis (Sullivan, 2005, 2010).

ABR disrupts ethnographies as well. Common to WS scholarship, good ethnographies provide insight and understanding in a more personalized way. They have been used since at least 1987, though at the time, Steven North, author of the landmark book on research methods, *The Making of Knowledge in Composition*, described them as "stories, fictions" written by composition researchers as ethnographers with "peculiar concern[s]" about individuals and the communities they are a part of (1987, p. 137). Decades later, Victor Villanueva (2011), drawing upon Ralph Cintron (1997), bell hooks 1990, and Linda Tuhiwai Smith (1999), pointed out the method's lack of credibility by identifying the racial biases present in the work of Mina Shaughnessy, and North's failure to see that "stories, fictions," authored by white researchers who attempt to fix the problems of poor student writers of color, for instance, are subjective. "Objective research just ain't possible in comp" (Villanueva, 2011, p. 122), and researchers must acknowledge their subjectivity—in fact, these truths, told alongside the "stories, fictions," are what make good ABR credible and vigorous.

Empirical, ethnographic, and arts-based research methods can be combined if a researcher wishes. By incorporating art at any stage of the research process, ABR projects can lead to new insights and engage researchers, research participants, and the general public in unexpected, equitable, and evocative ways. For example, art can be used to explore a research topic and identify and articulate a research question or problem; in exploring the topic, a researcher might create pottery or paint freely, letting emotional reactions to a personal concern, public crisis, or polemical topic guide their use of clay or brushstrokes toward a clear research question worthy of further investigation (see for example Franklin, 2013). Data collection can bridge conventional qualitative methods, such as an interview, with an arts-based approach. The possibilities for data analysis are numerous and evolving, such as collaborative analytical methods (Koski et al., 2016) or stumbling upon epiphanies latent in the data through the process of artistic creation (Sullivan, 2010). The roles of researchers and participants can converge. The researcher can become a participant-observer-artist involved in making art with participants, such as contributing to a mural, co-creating folk art, and choreographing or performing contemporary dance (see for example Saldaña, 2011). Participants can become researchers by, for instance, gathering data through photographs they take themselves; in turn they express themselves and challenge stereotypes, which can be transformative (Lenette, 2019; Oliviera, 2015). The art-making process provides WS researchers with experiential, immersive data consisting of authentic perspectives as well as venues where those perspectives, as research results, can be expressed in ways that are otherwise impossible. Art can be used to represent research (in the form of a novel, poem, painting, performance, etc.), present research (at a conference, art gallery, etc.), and re-present research (research reflection, typically appearing in a journal). ABR can be the product of a research project, the representational form as an artistic text. Researchers can learn, play, and experiment with new types of compositions as they express answers to a research problem. For researchers seeking to collaborate with their students, they can co-write poems, perform a play, or create and curate an art exhibit as ways to explore a research question; they can imagine and invent a vivid world that evokes empathy; they can express themselves in art-based ways that affect an audience and compels them to act, to change their perspectives, to relate, to feel less alone, or to incite new ideas for future research.

As I have touched upon, ABR has many techniques and benefits. They can lead to new personal and public understandings, epiphanies, closure or new openings, all of which can be personal to the researcher and beneficial to stakeholders in and beyond the discipline and geographical lines. They can create empathy. They can demand social justice and be socially just. If researchers have personal passions, such as playing an instrument or acting, they might find great fulfillment in discovering ways to incorporate these art forms into their work. ABR projects can connect with broader audiences who do not speak in academic terms, who cannot access language, or who simply enjoy the visual and performing arts. Research becomes entertainment that, if done well, can resonate with anyone. What is perhaps most exciting is that the methodologies are fluid, open to predetermined designs while also embracing failures, reconfigurations, and surprises. ABR can incorporate successful traditional research methods or rework prior approaches. ABR might even be a means by which WS can assert its status as a discipline by producing new disciplinary, interdisciplinary, and transdisciplinary knowledge relevant and applicable to academic and public contexts.

ABR in WS might be met with opposition and suspicion for at least two reasons. One possible source of opposition and suspicion is that, on the whole, artistic ways of knowing lack the credibility found in critical thinking as well as rigor lent in myriad citations; in consequence, it is frequently and erroneously dismissed in WS (Hanzalik, 2019). Furthermore, few WS journals are designed to accommodate arts-based texts, or what Doug Hesse refers to as "fully enact[ed] multimodality," "hypertext," and "nonlinear texts," which does not bode well for them (Hesse, 2019, p. 383). The scholarship published in emerging arts-based journals are written off by hiring committees and tenure and promotion committees as less important than the print-centric articles published in *College Composition and Communication* and *College English*. Anecdotally, WS dissertations that take an arts-based approach are often met with suspicion because they are perceived as lacking rigor, or they are dismissed as irrelevant to WS, even if they are widely celebrated in public life. Some suggest that WS must find its own signature research style (Massey and Gebhardt, 2011); however, I would argue that it is problematic to lay claim to a territory at a time when fields such as the visual and performing arts, social sciences, women's studies, healthcare, policy studies, and disabilities studies, to name a few, are deterritorializing and converging, learning from, and/or collaborating with each other as well as non-scholarly communities in ways that are useful and inciting—and ABR has played a major role in this shift. WS can advance ABR, which will further prove the strength, relevance, and importance of the discipline.

Art Across the Disciplines

ABR is taken up across and within a variety of disciplines. It has many analogues, such as PaR, RC, and a/r/tography. Each approach is worth knowing about, should researchers be drawn to different ones. All of them might inform the various purposes, topics, methodologies, and methods WS research can take.

PaR turns to art practice to find and create new understandings about any number of topics but particularly the human condition (see Nelson, 2013; Sullivan, 2005, 2010). PaR focuses on art making, the artist's process and practices in the studio, artistic ways of knowing from the perspective of the artist, and how they can use their crafts to build knowledge. Graeme Sullivan, a pioneer in the field, writes:

> Visual arts [is] a form of inquiry into the theories, practices, and contexts used by artists. The critical and creative investigations that occur in studios, galleries, on the Internet, in community space and in other places where artists work, are forms of research grounded in art practice.
>
> (2005, p. xi)

To Sullivan (2005), PaR is rigorous in the sense that it values "the role imagination and intellect plays in constructing knowledge that is not only new but has the capacity to transform human understanding" (p. xiii). Everything cannot be explained away, Sullivan contends (2005, 2010). PaR is not used to express a thesis but rather an exegesis (Sullivan, 2010, pp. 91–92):

> Understanding is as significant as an explanation as a goal of research, for understanding requires knowledge to be created from which explanations can be extracted: to create, the researcher has to enter the realm

> of imagination, to take the possible, as well as the plausible and probable. This practice is well known to artists and [literary] writers.
>
> (p. 115)

This knowledge can inspire WS to shift its focus away from calculated arguments, explanations, justification, and defense. Robin Nelson (2013), arts educator and performing arts and media scholar, argued, "PaR provides substantial insights rather than coming to such definite conclusions as to constitute answers" (p. 30). According to Nelson (2013), PaR bridges practice with theory to become praxis. Practitioners immerse themselves in an extemporaneous process of research rather than planning and implementing a research design (Nelson, 2013). Researchers might then be inspired to use their energy and efforts toward their inquiry to evoke, and be evoked, to embrace ambiguity rather than fear it, and to take pleasure in the playful practice of art making.

Arts education researchers, who are at once artists, teachers, and researchers, frequently use PaR to research and invent more inclusive pedagogical practices. One project that illustrates the benefits of a PaR is Kryssi Staikidis's *Kryssi Staikidis as Apprentice to Paula Nicho Cúmez* (2006). Concerned with the studio-arts education's preoccupation with kitsch and failure to remember that art is a cultural practice, the artist became an apprentice to two reputable Mayan artists, and under their guidance she created semi-abstract paintings that showcased an approach to studio-arts education that privileged traditional arts-education practices (Sullivan, 2010, p. 238). Staikidis argued that

> teaching structures that derive from indigenous artistic living traditions . . . would incorporate personal and cultural narrative, collaboration, negotiated curriculum, narrative dictation based on personal and cultural mythologies, the mental cataloging of stored visual information, and modified mentor/novice teaching systems that decentralize the teaching/learning experiences for students.
>
> (cited in Sullivan, 2010, p. 238)

Similarly, in the field of teacher education and other disciplines, researchers are increasingly taking up the genre of a/r/tography, which locates research in pedagogical spaces where educators as artist-researcher-teachers assume that arts practices are an important method of discovery and way of knowing that produces infinite important personal, collective, pedagogical, and epistemic insights (Irwin and De Cosson, 2004). A/r/tography is positioned in a "third space" or "borderlands," where the boundaries between the various roles that academics play are blurred (see Irwin and De Cosson, 2004).

RC combines research methods and artistic creation to create new understandings on any given topic and to subvert dominant approaches to research and art; definitions of research and art; and perceptions of, values for, and structures of disciplinarity, interdisciplinarity, and transdisciplinarity at the college level (see Loveless, 2019). Research-creation, as defined by the Social Sciences and Humanities Research Council of Canada, 2016, is "an approach to research that combines creative and academic research practices, and supports the development of knowledge and innovation through artistic expression, scholarly investigation, and experimentation" (as cited in Loveless, 2019, p. 6). The combination—research and creation—is not apolitical; it is intended as an intervention. To Natalie Loveless (2019), RC is a political tool—a way to enhance the status of artistic ways of knowing in the academy, but more importantly, to her, a way to reconfigure traditional disciplinary lines in the university, to change the education and output required of the professoriate and graduate students. RC is, she argued, "First and foremost . . . an urgent challenge to reigning pedagogical and research modalities and outputs in the university today" (p. 10). But it is also a way into self-expression and social critique. RC is "part research, part creation, part experiment that focuses on the output of the research" (p. 6). She argues that RC—given its innate interdisciplinary and transdisciplinary nature—can, as a doctoral degree, not only enhance the status of art in the academy but more importantly, reconfigure university traditions, academic departments, and the training of faculty and graduate students. Therefore, RC is especially useful for WS graduate students and faculty, and graduate programs more broadly. WS doctoral program directors might turn to RC for ideas about making the curriculum more interdisciplinary, forging new partnerships across the discipline in a way that leads to cross-listed, co-taught classes. It is about shaking up the university and innovating ideas and everyday expectations for professional life.

ABR is popular in many disciplines as a way of innovating research, engaging audiences, and inciting social change within and especially outside the academy. Fields such as therapy, educational research, and sociology, to name a few, appreciate ABR for different reasons, but it is unanimous that the approach is personally and professionally gratifying. In arts therapy, for instance, ABR is beneficial because it provides insight into the human condition (McNiff, 2013, p. 3) and presents new purposes and strategies for doing research, such as inspiring others, experiencing [artistic encounters], and building communities. This is important given the past, where art therapy research used psychological and social-scientific methods that denied the significance of the arts as a way of knowing, all for the purpose of demonstrating that the field is rigorous in the eyes of the academy (McNiff, 1998). An ABR project created by Michael Franklin, an artist and professor of arts therapy, demonstrates how deeply personal and gratifying ABR projects can be for the researcher while also being useful to the discipline (2013). Franklin turned to ABR when he was diagnosed with prostate cancer to contemplate questions such as: "Would I die? How would illness and treatment affect my manhood?" (p. 87). He was especially interested in advancing knowledge about contemplative arts therapy, so he chose meditation, clay, and charcoal as his media discovery. He noted, "Meditation helped me to witness my mind in action, while art allowed me to compassionately transmute the contents of my thoughts through the fire and earth materials of clay and charcoal" (p. 87). In his six-year process of creating 80 pots, he attempted to "become fluent in the metaphors of these materials," and gained new understandings and insights about himself and the "core sentiments" of ABR. He turned to ancient wisdom to conclude a present truth about ABR, which is that "turning attention inward and conscientiously exploring the diversity of our inner landscape would awaken human consciousness . . . through self-referential, autonomous, and egalitarian quality of images accessible through the arts, we can know and research layers of personal identity" (p. 85). WS scholars interested in exploring themes of embodiment, mindfulness, and emotional labor might find a similar arts-based approach both elucidating and healing.

ABR is important to education, where the term "arts-based research" is often used interchangeably with arts-based educational research (ABER) and scholartistry. Melisa "Misha" Cahnmann-Taylor, a widely published poet and language and literacy professor and researcher, and Richard Siegesmund, an internationally renowned arts educator, researcher, and artist, offer an eloquent perspective on why the arts matters in educational research:

> The arts promote shedding our conventional categorical labeling, and experiencing the smells, feelings, sounds, and sites of the world afresh. We feel our researcher-teacher-student bodies moving through space. It is a full attentiveness to the movement that counts, not our efficiency in reaching a predetermined destination.
>
> (2018, p. 5)

"Attentiveness" is evoked in Natalie LaBlanc's dissertation, a photographic essay about 16 abandoned schools. She used experimental photographic techniques, such as overexposure, blurring, and close-ups, and arranged the images and text fragments into five non-linear "concessions" in a way that "not only documents what is dis/appearing from the post industrial landscape, it also actively explores the generativity of loss and the possibilities of art as a form of remembrance, within a context shaped by history, power, and memory" (2018, p. 187). Part exploration, part exhibition, LeBlanc's project did not follow a "predetermined destination" (p. 187) but rather unfolded in a way that led to an exegesis that LeBlanc invited her audience to interpret themselves. WS scholars interested in researching the histories, material conditions, and disparities in composition classrooms, particularly now in light of a global pandemic and the current political terrain, might find LeBlanc's experimental photographic techniques and sites of research launching points for future research.

Quantitative, Qualitative, and Arts-Based Qualitative Research Paradigms

ABR is a product of the arts-based qualitative research paradigm, which has its roots in the qualitative and quantitative paradigms. The contentious debates surrounding the latter two paradigms suggests that the former might fit naturally in WS research methods.

Quantitative research uses numbers to test hypotheses and form new knowledge (Keyton, 2011). Valuing rigor, deductive reasoning, reliability (a consistent approach toward data collection that will lead to similar results in different contexts), and validity (an effective measure that results in accuracy), quantitative research attempts to objectively shed light on phenomena by posing a hypothesis that confirms or rejects a theory, or by posing a problem, and then systematically gathering and interpreting numerical data, such as statistics, that will lead to either a confirmation or rejection of a hypothesis or more in-depth insight into a problem (Keyton, 2011). Quantitative methods have numerous benefits: they are adopted across a range of disciplines as a research tradition, which cultivates stronger connections between disciplines; numbers and statistics make precise comparisons possible; quantitative research can accommodate large-scale studies, which results in more generalizable knowledge (Keyton, 2011). However, quantitative research is not always reliable, meaning the data is not collected in a consistent way nor capable of generating similar results in comparable studies; quantitative studies can also be invalid, meaning they cannot measure what they are supposed to measure (Keyton, 2011). There are also sociopolitical implications about the dangers of quantitative research, which resulted in the emergence of the qualitative paradigm. Researchers have challenged the quantitative paradigm, arguing that objectivity is impossible, data-driven approaches to understanding phenomena cannot capture the intricacies of human experience, and that by denying the subjective, the paradigm is denying the researcher's complex social reality and identity (Keyton, 2011; Leavy, 2009).

Qualitative research assumes knowledge is socially constructed (Keyton, 2011). Valuing credibility and triangulation (taking multiple approaches to studying a single research question or problem), it is a response to the emergence of critical theories pertaining to race, class, gender, sexual orientation, and abilities—all of which emphasized the importance of subjectivity and intersubjectivity (Keyton, 2011; Leavy, 2009). Qualitative research, like quantitative research, begins with a research question; then data is gathered by a researcher whose subjectivity and in-depth experience about what, how, and who is being studied leads to a greater understanding of subjective and intersubjective social reality. Rather than collecting surveys and calculating data to discover the facts, qualitative researchers' methods of data collection include participant-observations, interviews, focus groups, narrative analysis, and ethnography (Keyton, 2011). Qualitative research has its limitations; for example, the subjects of the research are not always easily accessible, the studies themselves are extensive and ongoing, or discoveries are not easy to generalize (Keyton, 2011).

In the early days of WS research, quantitative methods were common. While they are less common today (Haswell, 2005), quantitative methods are prevalent in particular avenues of WS research, such as second language and multilingual writing practices (Hesse, 2019). Richard Haswell argued that data-driven methods (Haswell, 2005, 2012), specifically replicable, aggregable, and data-supported (RAD) methods, are

> a best effort inquiry into the actualities of a situation, inquiry that is explicitly enough systematicized in sampling, execution, and analysis to be replicated; exactly enough circumscribed to be extended; and factually enough supported to be verified.
>
> (Haswell, 2012, p. 201)

The "actualities of a situation" discovered through a quantitative approach, scholars argued, are more accurate than hermeneutical approaches, which fail to understand the whole history, layers, and significance of data-driven research (Berkenkotter, 1989). Haswell (2012) argues that quantitative methods should not be subordinated because, as emails on the WS list-serve WPA-L show, they are frequently used by writing program administrators in need of data that would address programmatic goals. However, numerous researchers have critiqued the quantitative paradigm, acknowledging that the researcher's subjectivity influences problems posed, methods used, interpretations of findings, and the rhetorical nature of research more broadly (Bloom and Bloom, 1970; Firestone, 1987; Flynn, 1995; Villanueva, 2011).

In the 1980s, the arts-based paradigm emerged, with scholars challenging the quantitative and qualitative paradigms (Barone, 2006; Leavy, 2009). ABR research can combine qualitative, quantitative, and arts-based methods to discover and create understandings and affects rather than truth and knowledge. Like the qualitative paradigm, the arts-based qualitative paradigm assumes that the researcher is subjective; however, the contrasting assumption is that "knowledge [is] a process, a temporary state" (Eisner, 1997, as cited in Leavy, 2009, p. 9). Leavy writes that ABR was a new way of doing research that

> posed serious challenges to qualitative methods conventions, thus unsettling many assumptions about what constitutes research and knowledge . . . these disruptions to traditional research practices, much like early responses to the qualitative challenge to positivism have caused concerns and inspired debates . . . the emergence of arts-based social research advances critical conversations about the nature of social scientific practice and expands the borders of our methods repository.
>
> (p. 9)

ABR is not simply a new or different collection of more tools that can be added to a research project, however. Nor should it be viewed solely as a type of ethnography or as new hyphenated iterations of it (e.g., auto-ethnography, ethno-drama, ethno-poetry, etc.). Art is a powerful form of research on its own terms and when used in conjunction with the methods of other disciplines. As Leavy noted

> the tools shape topic selection, research questions and research design (from data collection to representation) . . . methodological innovation is not simply about adding new methods to our arsenal for the sake of "more" but rather opening up new ways to think about knowledge-building: new ways to see. Arts based research practices are about composing, weaving, and orchestrating—creating tapestries of meaning.
>
> (p. 254)

This applies to the diverse range of disciplines that are increasingly taking up ABR, all which desire new ways to see. While approaches within the arts-based qualitative paradigm might vary, they share common values and similar strengths. The arts are emotional and evocative; they create a sense of "immediacy" (p. 12), which captures the audience's attention. Scholars have written about how they are paths toward self-realization, how they raise critical consciousness, how they evoke, that they invite empathy, sympathy, and compassion while creating a sense of connection between audience, researcher, and participants (Alexander and Schlemmer, 2017; Bagley and Castro-Salazar, 2017; Eisner, 1997; Finley, 2017; Leavy, 2009; Lenette, 2019; McNiff, 1998), all of should be crucial to WS researchers.

Research deriving from the arts-based qualitative paradigm does not always begin with a research question that is answered in a systematic way. It might begin with a feeling, idea, or sense worth clarifying and exploring further through the arts without seeking an answer. There are some other differences as well. Whereas traditional qualitative research is made with words, writing, and "stories," as North (1987, p. 137) said, ABR is encompasses not only alphabetic texts but also "images, sounds, scenes, sensory" and "re (presenting)" (Leavy, 2009, p. 256). Whereas traditional ethnographic research is characterized by meaning, ABR is characterized by "evocation" (p. 256). Whereas traditional qualitative research is characterized by process, interpretation, and persuasion, ABR is characterized by authenticity and truthfulness (p. 256). And whereas traditional qualitative research is interdisciplinary, ABR is transdisciplinary (p. 256).

Leavy (2009) argued that ABR "allow[s] research questions to be posed in new ways, entirely new questions to be asked, and new non-academic audiences to be reached" (p. 12). ABR is not bound by academic language, and language more broadly, so it can reach a broader audience, which leads to greater possibilities for social change, challenges dominant ideologies and epistemologies, and creates a more inclusive society—all goals that drive a significant amount of WS research and pedagogy (Rappaport, 2013; Sakamoto, 2014).

As an academic language, ABR genuinely values and uses vernacular, speaks freely, expressively, and, if necessary, non-linearly—with humor sometimes and without jargon most times—all of which should interest WS scholars, particularly those who are interested in code-meshing (Young, 2010; Young and Martinez, 2011). And while ABR can be meshed with other methods, it is not yet another set of research techniques; rather, it is a way of perceiving the world (Leavy, 2009).

In WS, scholars have taken an arts-based approach, although not in those terms, specifically to challenge quantitative and qualitative research. For example, in his 2011 essay "Rhetoric, Racism, and the Remaking of Knowledge-making in Composition," Victor Villaneuva praised the mixed-genre critical autobiography because it subverted discriminatory, hegemonic research methods. He was intrigued by Eisner's 1981 article "On the Differences Between Scientific and Artistic Approaches to Qualitative Research," in which Eisner discusses how artists, such as filmmakers, make new knowledge through their artwork, but that it is impossible to evaluate the knowledge based on scientific standards such as validity and reliability. Villanueva (2011) appreciated the "illumination and penetration" made possible by artistic inquiry and viewed Eisner's wish to incorporate the arts into research as a rhetorical move. According to Villanueva:

> Eisner and others in educational research were making a case for research-as-rhetoric: persuasion, the credibility of the writer (ethos),

> time and place (kairos). That argument for those of us in composition would be most forcefully made by people of color. Although people of color were not the only ones making the shift to "artistically rendered research" (thinking here of Mike Rose as a popular mixed-genre, critical autobiographer of the later 1980s), it would be the writers of color who, by placing rhetorical strategies over scientistic ones, would feel compelled to underscore the continuing racism in our society and implicitly point to the continuing racism in what we do. People of color, addressing assimilation, addressing code switching, addressing forgotten histories, helping to change, instrumental in the change, in how we go about making knowledge in composition.
>
> (p. 126)

To Villanueva, ABR, recast as rhetoric, was a means of social change, a way to challenge assumptions about appropriate research methodologies. He recalls his 1993 book, *Bootstraps*, in which he uses ethnography, poetics, and rhetoric to challenge academic conventions. The arts informed the way he took a stance that had important implications for people of color whose subjectivities were treated like specimens for white WS scholars who failed to notice that research, from the subjects chosen to study to the methods of data collection and the way the data is interpreted, is not color blind.

Villaneuva perhaps unknowingly joined the arts-based qualitative paradigm. He uses the creative approach to research as a space for authentic expression that is not distorted by the requirements and codifications of conventional academic research and forms of representation. Villanueva's mixed-genre approach—using poetics, rhetoric, and ethnography—alter the expectations for the narrative genre, defying the ways genres force composers and the ideas and expressions to conform.

In response to dominant ways of knowing, composing, and teaching in WS, Victor Vitanza traveled alongside arts-based scholars in advocating for and performing new representational forms. Vitanza (1991) challenged WS's intention to "systematize (the) language (of composing)," "the will to be its authority," and "the will to teach its students" (p. 140). Vitanza also challenged "the game of rationality/knowledge" and the "dominant (political modes) of representation" (p. 143) in favor of "a game of art" that would aim to be, for instance, "random, and filled with fragmented thoughts and digressions . . . without knowing as a subject" (p. 165). The arts-based qualitative paradigm and ABR methods were taken up by Vitanza's confidant, Gregory Ulmer, who was especially critical of traditional logics of critique that privileged logocentric hermeneutics.

In 1983, Ulmer attended to historian and literary critic Hayden White's claim that scholars should "use *contemporary* scientific and artistic insights as methods of the basis for their work" (1978, as cited by Ulmer, 1983, p. 93). Criticism operated much like the logic of realism where close readings led to clear conjectures supported by evidence. However, as art moved from realism to modernism, White and Ulmer contended that criticism should change as well (1983). Like realism, traditional critical writing left no room for flights of fancy and ambiguities. In keeping with modernist art, however, Ulmer argued that scholars should move beyond criticism toward "post-criticism" by making collage/montages in response to texts (1983, p. 94). Ulmer encouraged researchers to ask: what can we make from the subject? A text made way to form and express an interpretation of that text in art form. In 1985, Ulmer expanded upon this arts-based approach by drawing from the philosophies of Jacques Derrida. His book, *Applied Grammatology*, challenged the power logocentrism had over pedagogy by turning to the logic of performance art, namely, the work of Joseph Bueys, and the logic of film, namely, Sergei Eisenstein (1985). With advancements in electronic media in the early 1990s, Ulmer's research advanced further as discussed in his book, *Heuretics* (1994).

Whereas post-criticism and applied grammatology concerned the representation of research, Ulmer envisioned the arts as a method (much like the scientific method) that would lead new discoveries. *Heuretics* (1994) seemed to allude to the heresy of his attempt to challenge heuristics. Ulmer was not dismissing conventional ways of knowing; rather, he was adding to it:

> Without relinquishing the presently established applications of theory in our disciplines (critic and hermeneutics), heuretics adds to these critical and interpretive practices a generative productivity of the sort practiced in the avant-garde. Vanguard artists, like their counterparts among academic critics today, often based their projects on the important theoretical texts of the day. The difference between the two applications has to do with their respective modes of representation: the artists demonstrate the consequences of the theories for the arts by practicing the arts themselves, generating models of prototypes that function critically as well as aesthetically. The vanguardist does not analyze existing art, but composes alternatives to it (or uses it as a step toward achieving alternatives.
>
> (p. xii)

His dynamic ideas for incorporating the arts into WS and pedagogy aligned with what was happening in the social sciences, art therapy, and education, to name a few. As ABR emerged in the social sciences, WS was concerned with challenging epistemologies, paradigms, practices, and assumptions and in turn advancing theories and practices for research and writing. Scholars who participated in what should be read as an arts-based movement did not identify as arts-based researchers, although their approaches, values, and methods thoroughly embodied ABR and anticipated its emergence in WS today.

The Arts-Based Writing Movement in WS

Arts-based turns in WS can be seen in doctoral programs, journals, and collections. For example, In the Rhetorics, Communication, and Information Design program at Clemson, A.D. Carson (2017), a doctoral student teaching first-year composition at the university from 2013 to 2017, produced a dissertation that was both written and arts-based, consisting of mixtapes that protested the denial of racist histories at Clemson and beyond. His work stretched the boundaries of WS as is traditionally understood, demonstrating that rapp (poetry and beats) is a form of scholarship, a pedagogy relevant to writing classrooms, and a method of social change.

Arts-based publishing can be found in Parlor Press's Electracy and Transmedia Studies Series and scholarly journals, such as *Textshop Experiments*. Corbett et al.'s (2019) *Writing in and About the Performing and Visual Arts* recalls a history of arts-based writing in scholarly journals as the impetus to the collection's visually appealing artistic texts that theorize and offer strategies for the teaching of art in composition classrooms and beyond. *Exquisite Corpse: Studio Arts-Based Writing in the Academy* (Hanzalik and Virgintino, 2019) incorporates arts-based research and writing to bridge conversations in WS about art and design pedagogies, electracy, and multimodal learning.

At St. John's Institute for Writing and Rhetoric, faculty, graduate students, and graduates are pushing boundaries and breaking new ground with pedagogies informed by art and design. The commonality among these scholars and texts is the recognition of art, on its own terms, in WS scholarship. This has resulted in vibrant ideas, interests, innovations, interest from audiences within and outside the academy, and the shaking up of virtual and physical academic spaces.

Some innovative scholars from St. John's include Nathalie Virgintino (2017), Hanzalik and Virgintino (2019), Vittoria Rubino (2019a, 2019b), Derek Owens (2019), Tara Roeder (2019; 2015, with Roseanne Gatto), Roseanne Gatto (2015, with Tara Roeder). Roseanne Gatto (2015, with Tara Roeder), and Megan Nolan (2019). Virgintino (in Hanzalik and Virgintino, 2019) speaks about the benefits of improvisation, arguing that a pedagogy informed by the improvisational practices of jazz musicians and dancers, for instance, can teach students new ways of looking at composing:

> As improvisation encourages experimentation with prior knowledge as a way of composing, failure will naturally occur. To guide students in

> becoming improvisatory writers and composers, we must discuss the meaning of success in the composition classroom, so that failure is not seen in a pejorative light, but rather welcomed and celebrated.
>
> (p. 183)

Moreover, Virgintino stated that improvisation in classrooms can address social problems such as universities with profit-minded missions that are best accomplished through what Henry Giroux refers to as a "pedagogy of conformity" (Giroux, 2014, as cited in Hanzalik and Virgintino, 2019, p. 177). Virgintino argued,

> Those using and theorizing improvisation in music, dance, and theater all recognize the need to develop a significant knowledge base, which resists the notion of accumulating and absorbing skills, conventions, and forms and instead pushes an improviser to select and interpret from them.
>
> (2019, p. 178)

In addition to setting the stage for ABR in WS, Rubino made the case that by adopting a "design disposition" in the composition classroom, "students can see composing as an exploratory, creative act of making and problem solving" (2019b, p. 146). Writing becomes a "design process," and pedagogy becomes "design-oriented" because it involves "diversifying our assignments, encouraging collaboration and discussion, and fostering an experimental yet structured approach to projects" (Rubino, 2019b, p. 146). Derek Owens (2019), artist and professor at St. John's University, described how the empathic critique that should be privileged in studio-art classes could be used in peer-review workshops in writing classrooms. He argued,

> Educators who have the privilege of choreographic spaces where students share their work with others (always a vulnerable situation) can learn from advocates for learning environments that value empathy over correction, play instead of punitive discipline, attention to students needs and motives more than unquestioned professorial judgement—and especially the welfare of the student's health and state of mind.
>
> (p. 218)

Also from St. John's University, poet and arts-based researcher Megan Nolan (2019) has written about how using poetry in composition classrooms can help writers to reconcile their fragmented identities.

Graduates from the Rhetorics, Communication, and Information Design Program at Clemson University have made important contributions to arts-based scholarship. A composition by Stowe and Rico (2019), "Write Your Title

Here," uses visual art as a form of representation and a subject of study in "Conversation Concerning Arts, Methods, and Some More." The authors' collage of alphabetic and non-alphabetic texts—scholarly citations laid out as poems; renderings of Rico's visual art (sketches, drafts in the studio, Instagram posts, finished versions pictured in a gallery or as a photograph)—explore and critique, in form and content, the composing process. The piece resists conventions of an academic text, such as stating and defending a thesis, explaining, using linear alphabetic prose, directly referring to and explaining the figures in the text to support an argument. In effect, the piece creates a sense of ambiguity, curiosity, and exigence that are hallmarks of ABR representational forms. Stowe and Rico's experimental style embodies the values and ideas of ABR. In addition to Carson's rapp album and traditional academic writing for his dissertation, "Owning My Masters: The Rhetorics of Rhymes and Revolutions" (2017), he published a "mixtap/e/essay" that addresses his history, African-American life, and manhood in a way that, as the University of Michigan Press describes, "performs hip-hop scholarship using sampled and live instrumentation; repurposed music, film, and news clips; and original rap lyrics" (2020a, 2020b). Carson's performance, which is free and accessible on the web, disrupts academic conventions, contributes to academic conversations, and reaches a non-academic audience.

In addition to doctoral programs and scholarly projects, scholarly conferences are emerging in support of the arts. For example, the 2019 State University of New York Conference on Writing was centered on "The Art of Writing/The Writing of Art." The event featured panel discussions by a diverse range of WS scholars and teachers as well as art critics, visual artists, literary artists, and performing artists to share pedagogical and scholarly practices that incorporates the arts. Virgintino and Hanzalik presented the keynote speech about how studio arts-based writing in the composition classroom can encourage risk taking and an appreciation for failure, challenge dangerous ideologies, and open new doors for transdisciplinary work.

Conclusion

WS researchers have reason to experiment with ABR. The field has a long and storied history debating about and experimenting with both the qualitative and quantitative paradigms. ABR offers researchers new and exciting ways to approach old, unanswered questions and explore current problems. In fact, WS scholars have been doing ABR to challenge the status quo, to protest against social injustices, and to create new possibilities for understanding and representing compositions. Researchers then should feel compelled to inquire more into ABR to determine if the approach is right for them.

Takeaways

- Arts-based research is a process by which scholars and/or their research participants engage the arts to shed light on a topic, problem, or question.
- The process of ABR can be wildly recursive or systematic; it can incorporate qualitative and/or qualitative methods, though it lends itself to projects that are expressly subjective as well as personal for the researcher and research participants.
- ABR standards of excellence include vigor instead of rigor, exegesis rather than thesis, and affect as credibility rather than validity and generalizability.
- The arts often lack credibility in WS, and are frequently recast in WS terms, such as multimodal compositions and literacy. However, as researchers seek new methods for addressing new and unresolved problems, they are taking more creative approaches that could be extended further to incorporate the arts.
- Some scholars, doctoral programs, and publishers have turned to the arts to innovate and/or to disrupt conventional, and at times, oppressive approaches to scholarship. Given the nature of the arts, ABR is especially useful for WS projects attending to public scholarship, community engagement, and social justice

References

Alexander, A., & Schlemmer, R. H. (2017). The convergence of critical pedagogy with arts-based service-learning. In R. Shin (Ed.), *Convergence of contemporary art, visual culture, and global civic engagement* (pp. 1–23). Hershey, PA: IGI Global.

Bagley, C., & Castro-Salazar, R. (2017). Critical arts-based research: A performance of provocation. *Qualitative Inquiry, 25*(2).

Banks, W. P., Cox, M. B., & Dadas, C. (Eds.). (2019). *Re/orienting writing studies: Queer methods, queer projects*. Boulder, CO: University Press of Colorado.

Barone, T. (2006). Guest editorial: Arts-based educational research then, now, and later. *Studies in Art Education, 48*(1), 4–8.

Barone, T., & Eisner, E. W. (1997). Arts-based educational research. In *Complementary methods for research in education* (pp. 73–98). Washington, DC: American Educational Research Association.

———. (2012). *Arts based research.* Los Angeles, CA: Sage Publications.

Bazerman, C., Dean, C. W., Early, J., Lunsford, K., Null, S., Rogers, P., & Stansell, A. (2012). *International advances in writing research: Cultures, places, measures*. Anderson, SC: Parlor Press.

Berkenkotter, C. (1989). The legacy of positivism in empirical composition research. *Journal of Advanced Composition, 9*(1/2), 69–82.

Bloom, L. Z., & Bloom, M. (1970). Of rats and men: Another plea for research in the teaching of English. *College English, 31*(8), 866.

Cahnmann-Taylor, M., & Siegesmund, R. (Eds.). (2018). *Arts-based research in education: Foundations for practice*. Abingdon, UK: Routledge.

Canagarajah, A. S. (2012). *Translingual practice: Global Englishes and cosmopolitan relations*. Milton Park, Abingdon, Oxon, and New York: Routledge. doi: 10.4324/9780203073889.

Carson, A. D. (2017). *Owning my masters: The rhetorics of rhymes & revolutions*. A dissertation for the graduate school at Clemson University. Phd.aydeethegreat.com.

———. (2020a). *I used to love to dream*. Ann Arbor, MI: University of Michigan Press. https://www.fulcrum.org/concern/monographs/m900nw52n.

———. (2020b). *Description: I used to love to dream*. Ann Arbor, MI: University of Michigan Press. https://www.press.umich.edu/11738372/i_used_to_love_to_dream.

Cintron, R. (1997). *Angels' town: Chero ways, gang life, and rhetorics of the everyday*. Boston, MA: Beacon.

Conference on College Composition and Communication. (2018). *Scholarship in rhetoric, writing, and composition: Guidelines for faculty, deans, and chairs* (2nd ed.). https://cccc.ncte.org/cccc/resources/positions/scholarshipincomp.

Corbett, S. J., LeMesurier, J. L., Decker, T. E., & Cooper, B. (Eds.). (2019). *Writing in and about the performing and visual arts: Creating, performing, and teaching.* Across the Disciplines Books. Fort Collins, CO: University Press of Colorado Press.

Eisner, E. (1981). On the differences between scientific and artistic approaches to qualitative research. *Educational Researcher, 10*(4), 5–9. https://doi.org/10.3102/0013189X010004005

———. (1997). The promise and perils of alternative forms of data representation. *Educational Researcher, 26*(6), 4–10.

Faulkner, S. L. (2016). The art of criteria: Ars criteria as demonstration of vigor in poetic inquiry. *Qualitative Inquiry, 22*(8), 662–665.

Finley, S. (2017). Arts-based research. In J. G. Knowles & A. L. Cole (Eds.), *Handbook of the arts in qualitative research: Perspectives, methodologies, examples, and issues* (pp. 72–82). Thousand Oaks, CA: Sage Publications.

Firestone, W. A. (1987). Meaning in method: The rhetoric of quantitative and qualitative research. *Educational Researcher, 16*(7), 16–21.

Flynn, E. (1995). Composition and scientism. *College Composition and Communication, 46*(3), 353–358.

Franklin, M. A. (2013). Know thyself: Awakening self-referential awareness through arts-based research. In S. McNiff (Ed.), *Art as research: Opportunities and challenges* (pp. 85–94). Bristol, UK: Intellect Books.

Frost, A., Kiernan, J., & Blum Malley, S. (Eds.). (2020). *Translingual dispositions: Globalized approaches to the teaching of writing*. International Exchanges on the Study of Writing. Boulder, CO: University Press of Colorado.

Grabill, J. T. (2012). Community-based research and the importance of a research stance. In L. Nickoson & M. P. Sheridan (Eds.), *Writing studies research in practice: Methods and methodologies* (pp. 210–219). Carbondale, IL: Southern Illinois University Press.

Haas, C., Takayoshi, P., & Carr, B. (2012). Analytic strategies, competent inquiries, and methodological tensions. In L. Nickoson & M. P. Sheridan (Eds.), *Writing studies research in practice: Methods and methodologies* (pp. 51–62). Carbondale, IL: Southern Illinois University Press.

Hanzalik, K. (2019). Creating art in a critical research and writing course. *Double Helix*, *7*, 1–16.

Hanzalik, K., & Virgintino, N. (2019). Social justice in (and beyond) the studio art-based classroom: Improvisation and play as responses to economic inequality. In K. Hanzalik & N. Virgintino (Eds.), *Exquisite corpse: Studio art-based writing in the academy* (pp. 173–196). Anderson, SC: Parlor Press.

Haswell, R. H. (2005). NCTE/CCCC's recent war on scholarship. *Written Communication*, *22*(2), 198–223.

———. (2012). Quantitative methods in composition studies: An introduction to their functionality. In L. Nickoson & M. P. Sheridan (Eds.), *Writing studies research in practice: Methods and methodologies* (pp. 185–196). Carbondale, IL: Southern Illinois University Press.

Hesse, D. (2019). Journals in composition studies, thirty-five years after. *College English*, *81*(4), 367–396.

hooks, b. (1990). *Yearning: Race, gender, and cultural politics*. Boston, MA: South End.

Inoue, A. B. (2012). Racial methodologies for composition studies: Reflecting on theories of race in writing assessment research. In L. Nickoson & M. P. Sheridan (Eds.), *Writing studies research in practice: Methods and methodologies* (pp. 135–149). Carbondale, IL: Southern Illinois University Press.

———. (2015). *Antiracist writing assessment ecologies: Teaching and assessing writing for a socially just future*. Anderson, SC: Parlor Press.

Irwin, R. L., & De Cosson, A. (Eds.). (2004). *A/r/tography: Rendering self through arts-based living inquiry*. Vancouver, CA: Pacific Educational Press.

Journet, D. (2012). Narrative turns in writing studies research. In L. Nickoson & M. P. Sheridan (Eds.), *Writing studies research in practice: Methods and methodologies* (pp. 13–24). Carbondale, IL: Southern Illinois University Press.

Keyton, J. (2011). *Communication research: Asking questions, finding answers*. New York, NY: McGraw-Hill Companies.

Koski, K., Heyning, F., & Zwijnenberg, R. (2016). Collaborative meaning-making in arts-based research: Data interpretation with an artist, a physician, and an art historian. *Art/Research International: A Transdisciplinary Journal*, *1*(1), 234–257.

Leavy, P. (Ed.). (2009). *Method meets art: Arts-based research practice*. New York, NY: Guilford Press.

LeBlanc, N. (2018). The abandoned school as an anomalous place of learning: A practice-led approach to doctoral research. In M. Cahnmann-Taylor & R. Seigesmund *Arts-based research in education* (pp. 174–189). Abingdon, UK: Routledge.

Lenette, C. (2019). *Arts-based methods in refugee research: Creating sanctuary*. Singapore: Springer.

Loveless, N. (2019). *How to make art at the end of the world: A manifesto for research-creation*. Durham, NC: Duke University Press.

Lunsford, A. (2012). Conducting writing research internationally. In L. Nickoson & M. P. Sheridan (Eds.), *Writing studies research in practice: Methods and methodologies* (pp. 220–230). Carbondale, IL: Southern Illinois University Press.

Massey, L., & Gephardt, R. C. (2011). *Changing of knowledge in composition: Contemporary perspectives*. Logan, UT: Utah State University Press.

McKee, H., & Porter, J. (2012). The ethics of conducting writing research on the internet: How heuristics help. In L. Nickoson & M. P. Sheridan (Eds.), *Writing studies research in practice: Methods and methodologies* (pp. 245–260). Carbondale, IL: Southern Illinois University Press.

McNiff, S. (1998). *Art-based research*. Philadelphia, PA: Jessica Kingsley Publishers.

———. (2008). Art-based research. In J. C. Knowles & A. L. Cole (Eds.), *Handbook of the arts in qualitative research: Perspectives, methodologies, examples, and issues* (pp. 29–40). Los Angeles : Sage Publications.

———. (2013). *Art as research: Opportunities and challenges*. Bristol, UK: Intellect Ltd.

Nelson, R. (2013). *Practice as research in the arts: Principles, protocols, pedagogies, resistances*. New York, NY: Palgrave Macmillan.

Nickoson, L. (2012). Revisiting composition research. In L. Nickoson & M. P. Sheridan (Eds.), *Writing studies research in practice: Methods and methodologies* (pp. 101–112). Carbondale, IL: Southern Illinois University Press.

Nolan, M. (2019). Multiplicity and the Student Writer. In K. Hanzalik & N. Virgintino (Eds.), *Exquisite corpse: Studio art-based writing in the academy* (pp. 222–243). Anderson, SC: Parlor Press.

North, S. M. (1987). *The making of knowledge in composition: Portrait of an emerging field*. Upper Montclair, NJ: Boynton and Cook Publishers.

Oliviera, E. (2015). MoVE (method: visual: explore): Marginalized migrant populations and the use of visual and narrative methodologies in South Africa. *Refugee Review: Re-Conceptualizing Refugees and Forced Migration in the 21st Century*, *1*, 34–48.

Owens, D. (2019). Workshops, critics, and the arts of response. In K. Hanzalik & N. Virgitino (Eds.), *Exquisite corpse: Studio art-based writing in the academy* (pp. 197–221). Anderson, SC: Parlor Press.

Poe, M., Inoue, A. B., & Elliot, N. (Eds.). (2018). Writing assessment, social justice, and the advancement of opportunity. In *Perspectives on writing*. Boulder, CO: University Press of Colorado.

Rappaport, L. (2013). Trusting the felt sense in art-based research. *Journal of Applied Arts & Health*, *4*(1), 97–104. doi: 10.1386/jaah.4.1.97_1.

Roeder, T. (2019). On composition and design. In K. Hanzalik & N. Virgintino (Eds.), *Exquisite corpse: Art-based writing practices in the academy* (pp. 123–124). Anderson, SC: Parlor Press.

Roeder, T., & Gatto, R. (Eds.). (2015). *Critical expressivism: Theory and practice in the composition classroom*. Anderson, SC: Parlor Press.

Rohan, L. (2012). Reseeing and redoing: Making historical research at the turn of the millennium. In L. Nickoson & M. P. Sheridan (Eds.), *Writing studies research in practice: Methods and methodologies* (pp. 25–35). Carbondale, IL: Southern Illinois University Press.

Rubino, V. S. (2019a). *The artistry of composition: Towards an arts-based pedagogy for first-year composition*. A dissertation for St. John's University, New York.

———. (2019b). The artistry of composition: Design thinking in writing studies. In K. Hanzalik & N. Virgintino (Eds.), *Exquisite corpse: Studio art-based writing in the academy* (pp. 125–148). Anderson, SC: Parlor Press.

Sakamoto, L. (2014). The use of the arts in promoting social justice. In M. Reisch (Ed.), *Routledge international handbook of social justice* (pp. 489–505). Abingdon, UK: Routledge.

Saldaña, J. (2011). *Ethnotheatre: Research from page to stage*. Walnut Creek, CA: Left Coast Press.

Schell, E. E., & Rawson, K. J. (Eds.). (2010). *Rhetorica in motion: Feminist rhetorical methods and methodologies*. Pittsburgh, PA: University of Pittsburgh Press.

Selfe, C. L., & Hawisher, G. E. (2012). Exceeding the bounds of the interview: Feminism, mediation, narrative, and conversations about digital literacy. In L. Nickoson & M. P. Sheridan (Eds.), *Writing studies research in practice: Methods and methodologies* (pp. 36–54). Carbondale, IL: Southern Illinois University Press.

Sheridan, M. P., & Nickoson, L. (2012). Introduction: Current conversations on writing research. In L. Nickoson & M. P. Sheridan (Eds.), *Writing studies research in practice: Methods and methodologies* (pp. 1–9). Carbondale, IL: Southern Illinois University Press.

Smith, L. T. (1999). *Decolonizing methodologies: Research and indigenous peoples*. London, UK: Zed and Dunedin.

Staikidis, K. (2006). Personal and cultural narrative as inspiration: A painting and pedagogical collaboration with Mayan artists. *Studies in Art Education, 47*(2), 118–138.

Stowe, S. A., & Rico, C. (2019). Write your title here: A conversation concerning arts, methods, and some more. In K. Hanzalik & N. Virgintino (Eds.), *Exquisite corpse: Studio art-based writing in the academy* (pp. 20–41). Anderson, SC: Parlor Press.

Sullivan, G. (2005). *Art practice as research: Inquiry in visual arts*. Thousand Oaks, CA: Sage Publications.

———. (2010). *Art practice as research: Inquiry in visual arts*. Thousand Oaks, CA: Sage Publications.

Ulmer, G. L. (1983). The object of post-criticism. In H. Foster (Ed.), *The anti-aesthetic: Essays on postmodern culture* (pp. 83–110). Port Townsend, WA: Bay Press.

———. (1985). *Applied grammatology: Post €-pedagogy from Jacques Derrida to Joseph Beuys*. Baltimore, MD: Johns Hopkins University Press.

———. (1994). *Heuretics: The logic of invention*. Baltimore, MD: Johns Hopkins University Press.

Villanueva Jr., V. (1993). *Bootstraps: From an American academic of color*. Urbana, IL: National Council of Teachers of English.

———. (2011). Rhetoric, racism, and the remaking of knowledge-making in composition. In L. Massey & R. C. Gephardt (Eds.), *Changing of knowledge in composition: Contemporary perspectives* (pp. 121–133). Logan, UT: Utah State University Press.

Virgintino, N. (2017). Improvisation and studio-based pedagogies in writing studies. A dissertation for St. John's University, New York.

Vitanza, V. J. (1991). Three countertheses: Or, a critical in (ter) vention into composition theories and pedagogies. In P. Harkin & J. Schilb (Eds.), *Contending with words: Composition and rhetoric in a postmodern age* (pp. 139–172). New York, NY: Modern Language Association.

White, H. V. (1978). *Tropics of discourse: Essays in cultural criticism*. Baltimore, MD: Johns Hopkins University Press.

Young, V. A. (2010). Should writers use they own English? *Iowa Journal of Cultural Studies*, *12*(1), 110–117.

Young, V. A., & Martinez, A. Y. (Eds.). (2011). *Code-meshing as world English: Pedagogy, policy, performance*. Urbana, IL: National Council of Teachers of English.

2 Motivations and Methods for Arts-Based Research

Why Do Arts-Based Research?

In a typical research project, a researcher attempts to find an appropriate methodology for a particular research question at hand. In this case, they might ask, what are the kinds of problems that ABR can effectively take up? Can ABR lead to the answers researchers are seeking? Am I seeking data that can reveal the truth of things? Am I seeking emotional, intimate accounts that provide nuance about social reality? These are all important questions inherent to empirical research—and ABR is good at addressing specific problems, gathering data that can be quantified, and producing narratives or accounts that reveal personal and/or collective experiences, given the strengths of the arts—but ABR operates somewhat differently from empirical research. ABR can be used to help a researcher identify a research problem or topic. ABR can lead to new understandings and affects instead of answers to research questions. ABR researchers might ask, what artistic genre could be useful in identifying and articulating the research question or problem? Who is my audience and what might appeal to them? Who do I want to compose with (myself, other academics or students, community members and interview subjects)? Is it gratifying to write academic journal articles and/or would I like to try something new? What type of genre am I interested in experimenting with?

The arts are good at challenging conventions and building new worlds. Barone and Eisner (2012) contend:

> Instead of contributing to the stability of prevailing assumptions about [important social and cultural] phenomena by (either explicitly through statement, argument, portraiture, or implicitly through silence or elision) reinforcing the conventional way of viewing them, the arts based researcher may persuade readers or percipients of the work (including the artist themselves) to revisit the world from a different direction,

> seeing it through fresh eyes, and thereby calling into question a singular, orthodox point of view point of view.
>
> (p. 16)

Scholars have identified numerous ways in which ABR is beneficial. ABR is said to be valuable for projects that do identity work; that address social problems, injustices, and stereotypes; and that aim for policy change (Finley, 2008; Irwin et al., 2009; Leavy, 2017; McIntyre, 2000). ABR can be used to inquire into the human condition and lived experiences of research participants who have been subjugated, marginalized, silenced, victimized, and traumatized (Green and Kloos, 2009; Kraehe and Brown, 2011; Leavy, 2009, 2017; Lenette, 2019; Oliviera, 2009). ABR is said to give people a voice (Finley, 2008, Lenette, 2019) and reach people in ways that are felt rather than language-centered (Rappaport, 2013). ABR shifts the power dynamics in research situations (Daniels, 2003); it is attributed with creating "critical awareness" and "raising consciousness" (Leavy, 2009, p. 13, 2017). Furthermore, ABR is good at capturing process, understanding the relations between the global, local, and individual, and exploring and expressing ambiguity (Leavy, 2017).

As it relates to WS, researchers working on projects that address discrimination at the levels of assessment, language, and rhetorical histories might turn to the arts to advance understanding of the topic, to further empathize, sympathize, and take strategic action. Because art can connect to a broader, non-academic audience in ways that traditional modes of scholarship cannot, WS scholars can use ABR to explore and speak out against social injustices, such as language discrimination or implicit biases in community literacy practices, to a diverse range of stakeholders, to engage the general public in conversations about these injustices, and to communicate strategies for action that a large audience might be willing to take because they are compelled to do so, not because it makes sense to do so. Whatever the motive(s), researchers should be open to risk-taking, imperfections, failure, and maybe even new friendships, as they design and implement their research plans.

Designing an Arts-Based Research Project

So how does one determine the way a research project should be taken up when using ABR? How should it be designed? Some argue that ABR can be systematic (McNiff, 2008), and some offer frameworks for situating research designs (Rolling, 2013; Sullivan, 2010). Sullivan (2010) contends that visual art PaR is recursive and ever-changing, a transformative process experienced by the researcher, who continually negotiates and shapes personal and theoretical viewpoints. In that sense, the beauty of ABR can be found in its fluidity; rather than developing a predetermined structure for interrogating a problem, an ABR methodology might develop, shift, change, and take lots of new shapes and directions as the project develops. ABR can be used at any stage of any research project. WS researchers should be excited to know that they can draw upon any number of methodologies (a research design for a specific project that derives from a research paradigm/paradigms or other metatheoretical perspectives) (Morrow and Brown, 1994) and methods (various tools that can be used as part of a methodology). Methods include tools that can be used to generate ideas, collect data (surveys, interviews, participant-observation), or represent research (novels, plays, films, journal articles) (Morrow and Brown, 1994). What I offer next is a set of methods and genres that researchers might want to draw upon to design their projects. I will then go on to describe the research design for my ABR project "The Artist's Process."

Methods

Researchers rely on arts-based methods as part of a broader arts-based methodology; they can incorporate ABR methods into a homegrown or mixed-method research project, and/or they can use an ABR method as a means of triangulation. All these approaches are useful to researchers seeking new, practical approaches to ethnography and/or ethnographic data collection. Here are a few examples of methods and some possible relevances to WS. It would be impossible to create an exhaustive list of methods in such a short book, but also in general. Readers should note that these methods originate from ABR, but one might also want to consider how WS methods can be revised with elements of ABR.

Image Elicitation Interview

In an image elicitation interview, the researcher presents a participant with an image and gives them the opportunity to respond to it. The image itself becomes the interview question, which provokes a different type of response, one that is more emotional and that derives from deep within the participant's psyche. The method is said to help participants to see themselves in a different light as well as create cross-cultural connections. Photos are typically used, but other artistic forms could be used as well (Harper, 2002). This approach might be useful for WS researchers interested in studying students' composing processes. Rather than asking students how they composed in a particular context, they might present them with an image that would cause the student to explain the experience of composing in that context. This would present the researcher with a less cognitive perspective and more in-depth perspective. Because the method has a pedagogical element to it (it is helping the participant to see themselves in a different light), the student might gain greater insight into who they are and the ways that intersect with how they compose. For further discussion and examples, see Glaw et al. (2017), Intke-Hernández and Holm (2015), and Holm et al. (2018).

Indigenous Storywork

Indigenous storywork is a method informed by Indigenous values, traditions, and beliefs where the interviewer (listener) approaches the interview subject (storyteller) with "The four Rs of respect, responsibility, reverence, reciprocity" and the intention to learn. The story that is crafted from the interview (which can be collaborative) is understood and interpreted by accounting for "*wholism, interrelatedness*, and *synergy*" (Archibald, 2008). As it relates to WS, this approach might be of interest to scholars who are interested in furthering research about multilingual writers. Multilingual writers are often spoken about/spoken for by an outsider who does not see the writers' valuable knowledge and cultural contexts. An indigenous storywork approach would allow the writer to share their valuable knowledge and speak for themselves in ways that teach researchers while simultaneously providing the participant the respect they deserve. This arts-based approach might then forge connections among writers across worlds and cultures. For further discussion and examples, see Archibald (2008).

Photovoice

For this method, research participants take their own pictures about the topic at hand. In doing so, the participants are given a voice on a subject that matters to them. The images incite dialogue, the subject's agency and connection with policymakers, and the opportunity for social change (Wang and Burris, 1997). This approach is useful to WS researchers who would like more participatory analysis of research. Researchers might want to take this for community-based research and research that is situated within the writing classroom. For WS scholars interested in emotional labor, photovoice is a way for educators and administrators to express their perspectives, experience, and emotions through their own pictures to incite dialogue and address problematic labor conditions. For further discussion and examples, see Latz (2017).

Portraiture

This approach bridges empirical and artistic methods in order to illustrate for academic and non-academic audiences the decency of a complex social world Lawrence-Lightfoot, 1997, in Lawrence-Lightfoot and Davis, 1997. Sara Lawrence-Lightfoot describes her process as exploring "the layers and subtexts of human experience; listening for the voices and silences, documenting the good, and honoring the chaos and contradictions, the ironies and ambiguities threaded through our lives" (Lawrence-Lightfoot, n.d.). The portraitist views research participants as valuable knowledge holders Lawrence-Lightfoot, 1997, in Lawrence-Lightfoot and Davis, 1997, and seeks out "convergent threads, illuminating metaphors, and overarching symbols" in the data that has been collected, as meaning is represented in narrative form (Lawrence-Lightfoot, 1997, in Lawrence-Lightfoot and Davis, 1997, p. 185). Lawrence-Lightfoot has used this method to create portraits of phenomena such as an institution, archeology, a concept, a relationship, a developmental stage, and a process (Lawrence-Lightfoot, n.d.). In WS, portraiture could be useful for institutional ethnography, process research, or participatory research about inclusivity in the classroom. For the latter, a researcher might ask undergraduate students to create portraitures of each other as a way to connect students who otherwise are disconnected from each other, which is particularly useful now as classrooms increasingly migrate online. This would present a way for them to see and write about the good in *each other*, as opposed to *the Other*. WS researchers might then analyze the portraitures, taking note of the "illuminating metaphors" in student writing, deriving meaning that can be theorized and shared in ways that address barriers and opportunities for inclusivity in (and beyond) the writing classroom.

Readers' Theater

In Readers' Theater, researchers form focus groups; members of the focus group and the researchers then become cast members in a play. They converse about a particular topic, which is the topic of the play. The discursive material from the discussion functions as data that can be analyzed and used to create and perform a drama (Norris, 2011). Instead of focus groups, researchers can consider conducting interviews and using excerpts from the interviews to form the drama (Finley, 2008). This method might be especially useful for WS scholars interested in researching graduate students (their research practices, educational experiences), where cohorts at a particular institution can serve as the focus group. This would give graduate students agency and a voice in the research process, beginning with data collection to data analysis and the representation of research in a way that is creative and elucidating for the researcher, particularly if they are seeking to collaborate with research participants. For further discussion and examples, see Donmoyer and Donmoyer (2008).

Response Art

This is an arts-based method used in art therapy where researchers attempt to develop a research project by composing visual art (Fish, 2012). This approach is versatile and can be used at any stage of the research process for a diverse range of research interests. It is particularly useful for single-authored research projects, but collaborative research approaches can benefit from response art as well. For further discussion and examples, see Fish (2019) and Gerge et al. (2017).

Genres

Table 2.1 lists some of the genres that can be used for ABR, their strengths, constraints, and examples to which WS researchers might want to refer. Please note, this is just a starting point, and WS researchers should feel compelled to make their own connections between their research interests and the capacities of each genre.

Researchers using ABR can select from among a wide variety of genres based on their goals with respect to the audience they wish to reach and other desired features, such as immediacy and the ability to convey emotion and other qualities, such as being compelling, surprising, shocking, engaging, or cathartic; the capacity to cultivate empathy, sympathy, compassion, or connection with the audience, researchers, and research participants; and the beauty in challenging conventional approaches toward research and conventional ways of knowing. Some of the challenges that are commonly discussed and debated concern how the project will be received by an audience and/or if it will be misunderstood (Findholt et al., 2011). Researchers disagree on whether a text needs an explainer that unpacks the meaning of the text; scholars frequently discuss the dangers of misrepresentation and unequal power dynamics between researcher and research participants. The question of technical mastery always looms in conversations about ABR, with some arguing that it is necessary if researchers want to affect their audiences (Barone and Eisner, 1997; Wood and Brown, 2011) others argue that researchers can be either experts or novices (Lawrence-Lightfoot and Davis, 1997), and some scholars argue that for community-engaged research, technical mastery is not as important as the dialogue made possible through artistic creation (Finley, 2008).

Table 2.1 Arts-based research genres, strengths and constraints, and examples and additional resources

Genre	*Strengths*	*Constraints*	*Examples and Additional Reading*
Literary Arts	*Fiction:* reaches a broad audience, conveys complex and detailed human experience, explains global/local/personal, evokes empathy; disrupts stereotypes and raises critical consciousness (Leavy, 2012, 2013, 2015, 2017); provides a layer of anonymity for participants (Marsh et al., 2017), offers truth in a way that cannot be otherwise expressed (Kalmanowitz, 2013); *poetry:* offers a creative way to express data (Faulkner, 2016); Carroll (2015) noted that poetry is therapeutic for the researcher, participants, and audience; that it is useful for those grappling with trauma; that it brings out inner wisdom; *Creative nonfiction:* evocatively ambiguous (Barone, 2008); *participatory writing/mixed-genre*: Schuler et al. (2016) found that it provides a space for marginalized voices and corrects stereotypes and that it is good at reaching a wide audience.	In fiction, truth, validity, and objectivity are difficult to demonstrate (Nayebzadah, 2016): presents new challenges for editorial evaluation and publication (Frank, 2000); poetry alone is not qualitative or quantitative and in turn struggles for legitimacy (Furman, 2006); creative nonfiction may be dismissed because of its ambiguity (Barone, 2008); for narrative more broadly, see Benson 2014.	Banks and Banks (1998); Leavy (2012, 2013, 2015) (fiction); Zhang (2018) (poetry); Richardson (1994) (poetry); Faulkner (2016) (poetry); Neilsen (2008) (mixed-genre); Sinner (2013) (creative nonfiction); Schuler et al. (2016) (participatory mixed-genre); Lenette et al. (2019) (digital storytelling).

(*Continued*)

Table 2.1 (Continued)

Genre	*Strengths*	*Constraints*	*Examples and Additional Reading*
Visual Arts	Good at generating ideas from research participants, presents new perspective to an audience, which can promote social change (Leavy, 2009); contributes to metacognitive awareness of composing process (Hanzalik, 2019); useful as a tool for analysis, knowledge creation/ data set (Lenette, 2019); promotes communication when the research and participants do not speak the same language (Holm, 2015, Holm et al., 2018; see also Holm, 2020).	If used irresponsibly, can perpetuate stereotypes (Leavy, 2009); although not required, an explainer or artist's statement can elucidate the artistic and critical thinking that shaped the visual art (Hanzalik, 2019); imagery could be misinterpreted (Lenette, 2019).	LeBlanc (2018) (photography); Ulmer (2019) (painting); Kuttner et al. (2017) and Sousanis (2018) (comics); Hanzalik (2019) (student art).
Performing Arts	Good at exploring identity constructs as an embodied, aesthetic, emotional experience; process of dancing leads to new actions and perceptions; particularly amenable to collaboration between researchers and research participants (Borovica, 2019; Fenge et al., 2016); provides a public space for marginalized people to express themselves in a way that cultivates empathy and teaches them new skills (Hodges et al., 2012, 2014); useful for audience engagement about public policy (Cox et al., 2009, as cited in Lenette, 2019).	Run the risk of asking too much of the research participants; for social-justice oriented, participatory performances intended to change policy, dialogues following the performance are often necessary; however, researchers must be vigilant about such factors as excluding people from the dialogue, how the discussion will take place, and what is discussed (Cox et al., 2009, as cited in Lenette, 2019).	Borovica (2019) (dance); Seen but Seldom Heard Project (performance poetry); Saldaña (2003, 2005, 2016) (plays/theatrical performances); Sanders (2006) (drama).

Music and Sound Art	Constructs meaning in a way that is not cognizable but rather felt; tells a story in a different way; can serve as a source of data collection; welcomes a multiplicity of voices (Daykin, 2009); distinctly powerful capacity to engage audience in a visceral way (Stoller, 1984; Bresler, 2008); flexible and fleeting (Bresler, 2008); therapeutic and empowering for participants (Lenette et al., 2019) disrupts optic interpretation, an ethical gesture toward alternate interpretive modes (Gershorn, 2019).	As a form of representation, music must be accompanied with an explainer or companion piece which unpacks the knowledge conveyed (Daykin, 2009); can be asking too much of research participants (Lenette, 2019).	Surman and De Johnette (2002); Carson (2017, 2020) (rapp); Seabrook (2017) (piano); *Rising from the Ashes* (hip hop) (Viega, 2016).
Film and Video	Useful for participatory research; gives research participant agency, especially in the recording and editing processes (Lenette, 2019); presents an opportunity to make use of technological capacities to create new meaning and "amplifies aspects of rhetorical devices" (B. Gaines, personal communication, 2020); invites researchers to express themselves and their research topic through creative techniques, conveys emotional resonances that can be analyzed in a way that conventional scholarly research methods cannot (Wood and Brown, 2011).	Risks inaccurately representing the research participants; technical knowledge necessary for the purposes of making and/or analyzing (Lenette, 2019); requires time and funding (Jones and Leavy, 2014); preoccupation with technology could reduce writing (B. Gaines, personal communication, 2020); risky to challenge conventional methods (Wood and Brown, 2011).	Bubb (2020), Gaines (2018), Jones (2014), Jones and Leavy (2014), *Lines of Flight*, Brown and Wood (2014).

Motivations and Methods of "The Artist's Process"

My ABR project, "The Artist's Process," was a study about the composing processes and contexts of former refugee artists. The project was intended to understand the affordances of ABR for our discipline. What can ABR methods tell us about the parallels between art and writing? How can it improve writing practices and research about writing? How might it advance the ways process is researched and documented? Beyond the discipline, a crucial question was, how can ABR contribute to disciplines and marginalized people beyond WS? In this case, how can it contribute to refugee artists, refugee and forced migration studies, and the limited research in immigration, migration, and the arts? And since a promise that ABR makes to the researcher is that the art produced through it can, at its core, be "personal, often intimate" (McNiff, 2012, p. 6) for the researcher, this study was also aimed at my own self-discovery. What can I learn about myself through ABR? Since ABR lends itself to "the problems of self-immersion," how can I "use these attributes to connect to others, the traditions of knowledge, and the current needs of our profession" (McNiff, 1998, p. 151)?

There are numerous reasons why the research questions are of pressing concern. First, although not foremost, artists can offer WS scholars new composing strategies, new perspectives on the connections between art and writing, and expert strategies and rhetorical choices that translate from art to writing; they can elucidate the way contexts inform composing processes, a concern for one of WS's eminent process researchers, Paul Prior, who notes, "We can only understand where texts come from . . . by careful tracing of their histories" (2004, p. 520). WS has a diverse range of tools for helping researchers "understand where texts come from"—think-aloud protocols (Prior, 2014, p. 505), retrospective accounts (2014, p. 509), semi-structured interviews (2014, p. 511), and simulated elicitation interviewing (2014, p. 513) to name a few—but these methods are outdated. Think-aloud protocols were discussed in 1981 by Flower and Hayes. Retrospective accounts date back to 1971 (see Emig, 1971); moreover, think-aloud protocols and retrospective accounts are not entirely accurate (Latif, 2019; Flower and Hayes, 1981; Tomlinson, 1984); they also assume process is traceable, an assumption challenged by scholars who argue that the writing process is not codifiable (see Dobrin et al., 2011). Shipka (2011) advocated for research that captures the processes of all different types of texts in different ways (e.g., video) over an extended duration of time. This project draws its inspiration from Shipka's call to action while advocating for process research that might serve broader purposes, disciplines, and people in addition to helping students to become better composers. The project was intended to see how ABR can enhance process research methods.

Second, many refugees are invisible and voiceless. Research in forced migration and refugee studies showed that there is an inadequate number of narratives from people with refugee backgrounds, which therefore silences voices and visibility and construes one voice, "the refugee voice" (Sigona, 2014). Nando Sigona (2014) asserted that this is due in part to the legal process of asylum-seeking, where documented stories must be configured according to a particular logic and focus, a rational, well-supported argument evincing truth, credibility, and individualized well-founded fear of persecution; another contributing factor is the way scholarship is done in refugee and forced migration studies, where theories and theoretical work about people from refugee backgrounds speak over, speak for, and interpret forced migrant voices. As Jay Marlowe (2018) argued, common narratives about refugees are those extraordinary stories that demonstrate and document traumatic experiences, and while elucidating and in some cases healing for the storytellers, these narratives can create a divide and contribute to Othering discourse in which refugees are perceived as victims who are different and powerless; he pointed out that everyday stories are the stories that go untold—those scenarios and situations that are more common and relatable. These might include, for example, navigating public systems ranging from public transportation to public assistance, to seeking employment, making friends, raising a family, enrolling children in schools, and celebrating cultural traditions. He argued that everyday stories establish affinities and offer an alternate to Othering discourse by demonstrating that people from refugee backgrounds are not individuals who have endured trauma but are dynamic and eclectic people who are capable of responding to trauma; everyday stories and extraordinary stories coalesce and enrich each other in such a way as to cultivate more positive resettlement experiences (2018). As Caroline Lenette (2019) pointed out, "we have a shared responsibility in our various roles as researchers, people with lived experiences, advocates, concerned citizens, practitioners and decision makers to redress some of the appalling situations resulting from forced migration" (p. 4), yet we also must point out the everyday situations and talents of those whose history is marred by egregious violence. This research project is intended to depict the everyday and the extraordinary and to identify how art mediates both.

Third, art empowers refugees and can change public perception and policy, although more research needs to be done (Martinello, 2015; Wright, 2014). What is known is that, according to curators, art critics, and scholars in immigration and the arts, art challenges "the refugee voice" or "the refugee image," where victims are either welcome or not, relatable or not, worthy of sympathy or suspicion and infectious, idolized or feared, pure or criminal (Fiddian-Qasmiyeh et al., 2014; Sigona, 2014; Wright, 2014). Terrence Wright argued that a positive media representation is a story about artistic traditions (Wright, 2014, p. 468). The voice and image—which play out in possibilities for refugees' artistic creation in the art world—influence and are influenced by political agendas (Martiniello, 2015). As such, it is important to see that what Alex Rotas (2004) and Sadfar Ahmed (2014) refer to as *refugee art* can have the capacity to be powerfully influential. Ahmed (2014) noticed through his work as a curator that when artists from refugee backgrounds have a platform to express themselves through their art, it is possible to challenge stereotypes and misunderstandings about the experiences of forced migration (p. 24). Refugee art presents authentic everyday/extraordinary stories that, Espiritu and Duong (2018) argued, offer "a crucial site of new forms of knowledge that would otherwise not be produced or shared" and reflect "social disorder and interruption" (p. 589). DiMaggio and Fernandez-Kelly (2015) examined how crossing borders impacted the purposes of artists from refugee backgrounds, the extent to which artists used (and can use) their art for cultural integration, upward mobility, and the institutions and organizations that create barriers and possibilities for artists; they also noted that, while inadequate, research about arts and immigration showed that composing is not an act of personal expression but is a social process influenced by and influencing legislation, policy, and economics. With more knowledge about this, research and refugee artists could have the capacity to influence policy (Lenette, 2019).

Fourth, the research provides participants with the much-needed space to be visible, to have a voice, to speak for themselves about their craft and the contexts informing them, to showcase their work as experts at their crafts, to document their stories, and to preserve their traditions and techniques. Sigona (2014) points out that books that memorialize refugee experiences, by bearing witness and preserving memories are important in building strong diasporic communities with "raw material" that comprise that memory that can be passed on to future generations (p. 376). This project can contribute to that memory.

According to Lenette (2019), research about refugees and forced migration produces predominantly "gender-blind" (p. 11) research: "Refugee women's perspectives are still underrepresented, leading to a paucity of research on gender-specific concerns, intersectional markers of identity and difference, and women's narratives of strengths, agency and resilience" (p. 23). One of the participants of this research project is a female artist from Syria. As such, this project can use ABR to advance knowledge about gendered and intersectional experience. ABR, Lenette (2019) argues, is an important method of disruption (p. 11) and one whose "ethical and collaborative methodologies can play a key role in fostering research spaces that offer sanctuary amid the complications of everyday life" (p. 3).

Finally, this project is important to me personally, for nostalgic reasons. I have an M.F.A. in writing from the Savannah College of Art and Design, where I studied creative nonfiction and art criticism, and an M.A. from Dartmouth College, where I studied fiction writing and comparative literature; this arts education, coupled with my time as a freelance feature writer and a once-published poet, helped me to reconcile my life. For many years, however, my writing has operated on the logic of justification (McNiff, 1998). As an editor of a scholarly collection about arts-based writing, an author of traditional and experimental scholarly journal articles, and a critical writing professor, I write according to and teach academic conventions. They do lead to insights and important knowledge, but I have tried my best not to lose sight of the fine arts as a form of knowledge. Similarly, for many years, I have tried my best not to forget my roots. I am a third-generation Italian American from Syracuse, New York, which is the site of the research. As my family grows older, and with my grandparents gone, what we have left are traditions, letters, recipes, photographs, antiques, memories, stories, and the city itself. The North Side, where my family lived and worked, has changed from an Italian neighborhood to one where thousands of former refugees have resettled after a life of hardship. Families from all over the world, such as Nepal, Burma, South Sudan, Ethiopia, Syria, the Democratic Republic of Congo, and Bosnia, have brought cultures and traditions to celebrate and share. I do not mourn the loss of the Italian neighborhood; in fact, I feel quite the opposite. I was interested in learning more about the people, places, and cultures of the present as a way to revisit and recontextualize my past, and I wanted to do so through the arts.

It was therefore important that I did my best to ensure that I used my self-inquiry to serve the research participants, scholarly disciplines, and greater good. My intention was to apply any self-realization made possible through this project to "connect to others, the traditions of knowledge, and the current needs of our profession" (McNiff, 1998, p. 151) and to collect and represent the knowledge, talent, stories, and traditions that these artists offer any reader who, for whatever reason, feels nostalgic.

ABR Methodology for "The Artist's Process"

Summary

My ABR methodology was designed to incorporate the arts in two ways and through one analytical framework. As a method of data collection, participants created art and shared stories (ethno-mimesis) in ways that included and drew upon modifications of think-aloud protocols (TAPs), a practice common to WS process researchers where participants speak out loud as they explain their processes, and retrospective interviews (RIs), another method of process research where composers reflect on their composing process after a composition is done. I analyzed the data using Marlowe's concurrent everyday and extraordinary analysis as previously described (2018, p. 36). The intended plan was to represent the data as an enhanced process narrative common to WS, specifically the artistic impressionistic autoethnography (scholarly, evocative, first-person narrative recounting a social phenomenon) as a short story (non-scholarly first-person experience capturing the artist's process using literary devices).

Data Collection: Ethno-Mimesis

Data was collected through ethno-mimesis, an approach to research with/about people from refugee backgrounds specifically (O'Neill, 2008). Ethnographers typically conduct life story interviews; participants share stories about home, identity, belonging, and experiences in the context of forced migration; and artists collaborate to represent those stories in art form (O'Neill, 2008). According to Maggie O'Neill (2008), "The inter-textuality of biography/narrative (ethnography) and art (mimesis) becomes a potential space for transformative possibilities" (n.p.). Both art and biography/narrative are subversive in the sense that they are insider perspectives. They challenge stereotypes, give the participants space to speak for themselves, to raise their voices and visibility. The combination, "the mimetic re-telling of life narratives in artistic form," is useful for "capturing more sensuous meanings and experiences including memories, experiences, associations—indeed, all the senses involved in narration" (n.p.). Participants do not have to be artists. Artists can be brought into the research setting, but my project was unique in that the participants were artists and they had already started their mimeses, art, compositions. O'Neill describes a project where she collaborated with Bosnians and a community arts organization and learned about the participants through life-story interviews (2019). Regarding my project, during the life-story interviews, I asked questions about their values, families, communities, art practices, and, through that, their experiences and challenges from being a refugee to asylum-seeking and resettlement. In keeping with O'Neill's ethno-mimesis approach, the answers to the questions were intended to make the participants visible, to give them the space to express their voices and share their everyday and extraordinary experiences that may challenge stereotypes and invite readers to identify with rather than identify people from refugee backgrounds as Other. In turn, the goal was to learn about their experiences of resettlement in relation to my own family's resettlement.

As part of the ethno-mimesis, the TAPs followed the life-story interviews. They were intended to document the artists' composing processes and rhetorical choices. Generally speaking, the TAP method asks participants to explain their processes, decisions, and thoughts about their strategies as they compose (Flower and Hayes, 1981; Latif, 2019). However, they have their limits. Specifically, the researcher cannot capture an authentic perspective of the composing process because the research typically takes place in an institutional setting (Flower and Hayes, 1981; Smagorinsky, 1994), and the method is not conversational (Flower and Hayes, 1981), among other limitations (see Latif, 2019). Given the nature and purposes of the ethno-mimeses, I wanted to use the TAP to "facilitate expression" (O'Neill, 2008, n.p.) about more personal matters and in doing so enhance the capacities of the TAP. Requiring artists to speak solely about composing in an unfamiliar setting seemed less useful as well as inaccurate and limiting. To facilitate expression, the TAPs took place as more of a conversation in locations where the artists typically compose rather than in an institutional setting.

TAPs for this project were intended to identify the artists' rhetorical choices, to elicit a dialogue and an explanation of how they were making what they were making, and to talk with them about anything else they wanted to mention. I asked questions such as, what goes through your mind as you compose? Other questions had to do with purpose and decisions. Why are you creating this piece of art? Why did you make this particular decision (e.g., the choice of paint color or a particular pattern)? What guides your decision making as you compose? Tradition? Personal expression? Making sure the work is of a certain quality that the audience would appreciate? I was also interested in how the participants viewed problem-solving, since problem-solving is an important topic of research in arts-based writing (see Marback, 2009; Rubino, 2019). I wanted to find out what they considered to be problems, barriers, stoppages, or blockages in their composition that must be fixed and how they were fixed. These questions matter considering their expertise and their transnational pasts, presents, and futures that involved significant problems and obstacles. In this way, their processes of art making would reveal their character.

The TAPs were followed up with retrospective interviews (RIs), also common to writing process researchers and writing students, where participants reflect on their processes and finished product after the art has been created. Like the TAP method, the project specifically locates RIs as part of the ethno-mimesis, in turn revising ABR methods and repurposing WS methods. RIs, which can be considered another genre of the reflection, are common research and pedagogical tools in the field of WS, although the field is advocating for more research and better methods (see Latif, 2019; Prior, 2004; Shipka, 2011). RIs, also referred to as introspective analysis or retrospective analysis, are critiqued because they are inaccurate, they sometimes state what the composer should have done rather than what they actually did, and oftentimes aspects of composing are inarticulable (Flower and Hayes, 1981); moreover, composers cannot easily remember all the details (Tomlinson, 1984), and the method does not adequately account for context. For example, Scott (2009) rethinks writing about writing as not simply as an act of looking back at the process, remembering and recounting it, or even remembering it in a context, but rather re-seeing the process as part of a broader inequitable political-economic context.

To address those limitations in light of the ethno-mimesis, the RI method for my study became a space for open-ended questions that encouraged reflection about anything the artists wanted to discuss after they finished the composition, as well as their evaluations of the composition. To further our understanding of the parallels between art and writing and how expert artists judge their own work, Peter Elbow (1993) pointed out two common methods are evaluation (identifying the strengths and weaknesses) and liking (which would lead to an optimistic approach toward revision). He argued that liking is more productive (Elbow, 1993). I was interested in finding out if the participants evaluate and/or like or dislike, what the basis of their judgment was, and if they judge their work more than themselves or both equally or not at all. To that end, I asked them to respond to questions, such as "did you encounter any problems creating this project?" "If so, how did you overcome it?" "Did the piece turn out the way you wanted it to?" "What are your thoughts about what you made and your experience making it?" The RAs were optional so as not to burden the participants and required correspondence sometime after the TAPs.

Finally, in keeping with ethno-mimesis, I also accounted for the artists' artwork as part of the data set as a way to shed further light on the artist (i.e., the art becomes a part of the artist's biography) (O'Neill, 2008), their artistic styles, expressions, and traditions alongside the experiences of forced migration and transnational resettlement.

Data Analysis: Everyday/Extraordinary Framework

Patricia Leavy (2009) encouraged scholars interested in ABR to ask themselves, "How will I use theory? How will I employ theoretical lenses that operate on different levels, as well as those that may differ from my first inclinations?" (p. 50). The frame for this project was Marlowe's (2018) concurrent everyday and extraordinary analysis (p. 36), which is intended to correct misperceptions of former refugees, provide space for emic narratives that shed light not only on the experiences of the past, the dynamic processes of resettlement, and the realities of everyday life. The analytical frame is particularly useful for this project because it is broad enough to allow for an open inquiry into the artist's everyday composing processes.

Data Representation: Impressionistic Autoethnography as Short Story

The data was intended to be showcased, represented, through an impressionistic autoethnograpy, which Leavy (2009) defines as "an emergent method that is generally used in ethnographic research, thereby merging data about the others and the self" (p. 38). The genre is described as "figurative, personalized, fleeting, dramatic, and part realist/confessional" (Van Maanen, 1988, as cited in Skinner, 2003, p. 514). As mentioned, WS scholars might view the genre as an enhanced process narrative, specifically a short story, a way of narrating that intertwines the stories of interview subjects as they compose and the researcher as narrator to tell a nonfiction story that uses the techniques of fiction. I chose this method in part because it lends itself to personal reflection, emotion, and portraying the nuances of a social reality that always seems to be fleeting. The intended plan was to not use scholarly conventions for formatting and language (e.g., parenthetical documentation, use of jargon) in order to connect with a broader audience and make the piece genuinely artistic.

Study Participants

Congolese Fabric Artist and Syrian Visual Artist and Poet—Experts of Their Craft

The participants included two fabric artists from refugee backgrounds, both experts of their craft. Mmalanibwa LoseLose is a fabric artist from the Democratic Republic of Congo. Nada Odeh is a visual artist and poet from Syria. They have different experiences with war, encampment, asylum seeking, and resettlement. They also compose their art forms for different purposes, audiences, and, ultimately, rhetorical situations to which the story intended to explore. Rather than starting new projects for the purpose of the study, the study focused on projects the artists had already begun. LoseLose had already created a draft of the project and was in the early stages of embroidering. Odeh was working on *We Are Immigrants*, a series of four canvas paintings that was collaboratively made with Syracuse residents, including new Americans and those whose families immigrated to the United States many years ago.

Research Site

A Sanctuary City—Syracuse, New York

The study took place in Syracuse, New York. Syracuse has been described as "a city known for the resettlement of people who fled their home countries in fear of persecution over religion, race, or membership in a social group" (Breidenbach, 2018). It is classified as a Sanctuary City, a place where people can, regardless of citizenship status, obtain employment opportunities, housing, education, and health care without living in fear of deportation, forced separation from their families, and imprisonment (Baker, 2017; Sanctuary Policies: An Overview, 2017). Because former refugees are legal immigrants, sanctuary policies within a city do not necessarily apply. Although, if, for instance, a former refugee is seeking language-learning classes, a sanctuary city ensures these classes are available to all. In Syracuse, former refugees navigate a complicated economic, social, and political landscape. The terms "former refugee" or "refugee" have been replaced with "new American" because new Americans are already citizens, and the term refugee casts them as Other (New American Forum). All of this information was integral to and included in the story.

Numerous resettlement agencies in Syracuse have worked with refugees abroad to secure housing for them based on the needs and interests of the families; they pick refuges up at the airport, provide them with groceries, assist them in finding and preparing for job interviews, signing up for public assistance, enrolling children in schools, and directing families to language classes (Center for New Americans, 2020). However, President Trump's ban on travel from Muslim countries and attack on Sanctuary Cities resulted in cuts to federal funding and a 72 percent reduction in the arrival of new Americans, which has impacted the agencies (Breidenbach, 2018). In terms of economics, the city is emerging from a poverty crisis, what some call a "crisis of misery," with more than 50 percent of Latinx and Asian residents living below the poverty line (Eisenstadt, 2016). Eisenstadt (2016) noted, "You can see the impact of this pain in Syracuse's struggles to teach its youth, stay healthy, remain safe and promote hope of a better day." By 2019, however, the economy in Syracuse and the surrounding suburbs was "far outpacing other upstate [New York] cities" (Bolt, 2020).

In the media, new Americans have often been portrayed only in relation to their traumatic experiences and their cultural and economic contributions to Syracuse. Stephanie Miner, the city's former mayor, was quoted in the local newspaper saying they are "economic engines" (Miner as cited in Baker, 2016). Residents have commented that Miner is "purely an idiot [who] . . . would rather put the Real Citizens of Syracuse in Harm's Way" (Chuckyray1 as cited in Baker, 2017). Some say that refugees will increase competition among low-skilled workers (Lightn1 as cited in Baker, 2017) and that they are "draining society" (Who Really Cares Anyway cited in Breidenbach, 2018). Chris Baker, a reporter for Syracuse.com, explains that "refugees represent a long-term investment in the city's future—an up-front expense that often yields successful citizens" (2016). The media presents extraordinary stories of New Americans, such as asylum narratives that shed light on the traumatic experiences of New Americans (Tulloch, 2018); they also present everyday stories about the traditions and businesses of New Americans (Porcelli, 2017).

Within that context, the ethno-mimeses and TAPs were conducted at different locations familiar to the participants. For LoseLose, it was at the Congolese Women's Empowerment Sewing Group workshop at St. Stephen's Church on the North Side of Syracuse. For Odeh, it was in the basement art studio of her home in a suburban town near Syracuse.

Conclusion

As this chapter has detailed, there are numerous reasons why a researcher might want to take up ABR. There are a diverse range of methods to draw upon. They can be incorporated at any stage of a research process, and oftentimes ABR methods can be combined with empirical methods. Different art forms have different strengths and limitations; commonly, the arts have the capacity to portray worlds and evoke emotions. My research design posed questions intended to shed light on the parallels between WS and art, the ways ABR and conventional WS research methods can be combined, the experiences of people from refugee backgrounds, including female artists, and how everyday/extraordinary stories, made possible through ABR (ethno-mimesis and impressionistic autoethnography), can be used to serve the greater good, challenge stereotypes, engage in dialogue, and serve the research participants and the researcher.

The next chapter sheds light on the process of representing ABR research more broadly and showcases my research in art form. The fourth chapter discusses the important practice of methodological disclosure, which is to say reflecting on the research methodology. I discuss different ways to go about methodological disclosure and present my own, where I report my research results and process, acknowledge my subjectivity, and discuss ethics in relation to aesthetic decisions and engagement with research participants. Throughout the chapter, I touch upon limits to ABR and conclude with a brief discussion about the challenges and implications of assessment. The final chapter provides recommendations and ideas for future research and pedagogical applications.

Takeaways

- Determining if ABR is right for the researcher does not depend solely on validity but on credibility and the researcher's curiosity about which art form(s) they might want to experiment with and compose within to research the topic and inquire into their own lives.
- ABR projects play off the strengths of the arts. It lends itself to participatory projects; it can connect with the general public; it lets the researcher feel more personally invested in the research project; it can be a method of resisting social injustices; it builds worlds, sheds light on processes, and draws connections between theories and realities. Each genre has strengths and constraints.
- Researchers can design their projects by taking an interdisciplinary approach to data collection that builds off the strengths of traditional methods and possibly enhances them through the arts, although the design is likely to change as the project progresses.

References

Ahmed, S. (2014). Bearing witness: The refugee art project. *Art Monthly Australia* (272), 24.

Archibald, J. A. (2008). An indigenous storywork methodology. In J. G. Knowles & A. L. Cole (Eds.), *Handbook of the arts in qualitative research: Perspectives, methodologies, examples, and issues* (pp. 371–393). Los Angeles, CA: Sage Publications.

Baker, C. (2016b, March 14). Refugees in Syracuse: Benefit or burden? Here's what the numbers say. *Syracuse.com*. Retrieved from https://www.syracuse.com/poverty/2016/03/refugees_in_syracuse_benefit_burden.html

———. (2017). Is Syracuse a sanctuary city? Can Trump pull federal funds? 6 answers about immigration policy. *Syracuse.com*. https://www.syracuse.com/news/2017/01/is_syracuse_a_sanctuary_city_will_trump_pull_federal_funds_6_qs_and_as_about_imm.html.

Banks, A., & Banks, S. P. (Eds.). (1998). *Fiction and social research: By ice or fire*. Lanham, MD: AltaMira Press.

Banks, S. (2008). Writing as theory: In defense of fiction. In J. G. Knowles & A. L. Cole (Eds.), *Handbook of the arts in qualitative research: Perspectives, methodologies, examples, and issues* (pp. 155–165). Thousand Oaks, CA: Sage Publications.

Barone, T., & Eisner, E. W. (2012). *Arts based research*. Los Angeles: Sage Publications.

Barone, T., & Eisner, E. W. (1997). Arts-based educational research. *In Complementary methods for research in education* (pp. 73–98). Washington, DC: American Educational Research Association.

Benson, P. (2014). Narrative inquiry in applied linguistics research. *Annual Review of Applied Linguistics*, *34*, 154–170.

Breidenbach, M. (2018). New refugees drop 72 percent in Syracuse area in Trump's first year: A 10-year low. *Syracuse.com*. https://www.syracuse.com/state/2018/01/

refugee_arrivals_drop_72_percent_in_onondaga_county_during_trumps_first_year.html#:~:text=New%20York%20State-,New%20refugees%20drop%2072%20percent%20in%20Syracuse%20area%20in,year%3B%20a%2010%2Dyear%20low&text=Syracuse%2C%20N.Y.,percent%20from%201%2C466%20in%202016.

Bresler, L. (2008). Arts-based research and drama education. In S. Schonmann (Ed.), *Key concepts in theatre/drama education* (pp. 319–326). Boston, MA: Sense Publishers.

Brown, S., & Wood, M. (2014). *Lines of flight*. Best newcomer short. Iafor: Asia's think tank. Youtube. https://www.youtube.com/watch?v=sc8yz1RPeYc.

Bolt, C. (2020, Jan. 14). Syracuse region economy growth far outpacing other upstate cities: 2019 centerstate CEO data. *WAER*. https://www.waer.org/post/syracuse-region-economy-growth-far-outpacing-other-upstate-cities-2019-centerstate-ceo-data

Bondo. (2017, Feb. 9). Comment on Allen, P. & Breidenbach, M. Refugees in Onondaga County: Where are they from? When did they arrive? *Syracuse.com*. www.syracuse.com/news/2017/02/refugees_in_onondaga_county_where_are_they_from_when_did_they_arrive_1.html.

Borovica, T. (2019). Dance as a way of knowing: A creative inquiry into the embodiment of womanhood through dance. *Leisure Studies*, *39*(4), 1–12. doi: 10.1080/02614367.2019.1663442..

Bubb, J. (2020). The missing page: Place as palimpsest and "foil". *Journal for Artistic Research*, *20*.

Carson, A. D. (2017). *Owning my masters: The rhetorics of rhymes & revolutions*. A dissertation for Clemson University. phd.aydeethegreat.com.

———. (2020). *I used to love to dream*. Ann Arbor, MI: University of Michigan Press. https://www.fulcrum.org/concern/monographs/m900nw52n.

Chuckyray1 (2017, Jan. 25). In C. Baker, Is Syracuse a sanctuary city? Can Trump pull federal funds? 6 answers about immigration policy. *Syracuse.com*. https://www.syracuse.com/news/2017/01/i.

Center for New Americans (2020). Resettlement services. *Interfaith Works*. https://www.interfaithworkscny.org/programs/center-for-new-americans-2-3-2/.

Cox, S. M., Kazubowski-Houston, M., & Nisker, J. (2009). Genetics on stage: Public engagement in health policy development on preimplantation genetic diagnosis. *Social Science & Medicine (1982)*, *68*(8), 1472–1480. doi: 10.1016/j.socscimed.2009.01.044.

Daniels, D. (2003). Learning about community leadership: Fusing methodology and pedagogy to learn about the lives of settlement women. *Adult Education Quarterly*, *53*(3), 189–206.

Daykin, N. (2009). The role of music in arts-based qualitative inquiry. In P. Leavy (Ed.), *Method meets art: Social research and the creative arts*. New York, NY: Guilford Press.

de Freitas, E. (2003). Contested positions: How fiction informs empathetic research. *International Journal of Education and the Arts*, *4*(7). www.ijea.org/v4n7.

———. (2004). Reclaiming rigour as trust: The playful process of writing fiction. In A. L. Cole, L. Neilsen, J. G. Knowles, & T. C. Luciani (Eds.), *Provoked by art: Theorizing arts-informed research* (pp. 262–272). Halifax, NS, Canada: Backalong Books.

———. (2008). Bad intentions: Using fiction to interrogate research intentions. *Educational Insights*, *12*(1). www/ccfi.educ.ubc.ca/publication/insights/v12n01/articles/defreitas/index.html.

DiMaggio, P., & Fernandez-Kelly, P. (2015). Immigration and the arts: A theoretical inquiry. *Ethnic and Racial Studies*, *38*(8), 1236–1244.

Dobrin, S. I., Rice, J. A., & Vastola, M. (2011). *Beyond postprocess*. Logan, UT: Utah State University Press.

Donmoyer, R., & Donmoyer, J. (2008). Readers' theater as a data display strategy. In J. G. Knowles & A. L. Cole (Eds.), *Handbook of the arts in qualitative research: Perspectives, methodologies, examples, and issues* (pp. 209–225). Thousand Oaks, CA: Sage Publications.

Eisenstadt, M. (2016, Mar. 10). The cost of poverty: Syracuse's crisis of misery touches all parts of life here. *Syracuse.com*. https://www.syracuse.com/news/2016/03/syracuses_high_concentration_of_poverty_touches_all_facets_of_life_in_the_city.html.

Elbow, P. (1993). Ranking, evaluating, and liking: Sorting out three forms of judgment. *College English*, *55*(2), 187–206.

Emig, J. A. (1971). *The composing processes of twelfth graders*. Urbana, IL: National Council of Teachers of English.

Espiritu, Y. L., & Duong, L. (2018). Feminist refugee epistemology: Reading displacement in Vietnamese and Syrian refugee art. *Signs: Journal of Women in Culture and Society*, *43*(3), 587–615.

Faulkner, S. L. (2016). *Poetry as method: Reporting research through verse*. Abingdon, UK: Routledge.

Fiddian-Qasmiyeh, E., Loesher, G., Long, K., & Signona, N. (Eds.). (2014). Introduction. In *The Oxford handbook of refugee and forced migration studies* (1st ed., pp. 1–19). Oxford, UK: Oxford University Press.

Findholt, N. E., Michael, Y. L., & Davis, M. M. (2011). Photovoice engages rural youth in childhood obesity prevention. *Public Health Nursing*, *28*(2), 186–192.

Finley, S. (2008). Arts-based research. In J. G. Knowles & A. L. Cole (Eds.), *Handbook of the arts in qualitative research* (pp. 71–81). Los Angeles, CA: Sage Publications.

Fish, B. J. (2012). Response art: The art of the art therapist. *Art Therapy*, *29*(3), 138–143. doi: 10.1080/07421656.2012.701594.

———. (2019). Response art in art therapy: Historical and contemporary overview. *Art Therapy*, *36*(3), 122–132. doi: 10.1080/07421656.2019.1648915.

Flower, L., & Hayes, J. (1981). A cognitive process theory of writing. *College Composition and Communication*, *32*(4), 365–387.

Furman, R. (2006). Poetry as research: Advancing scholarship and the development of poetry therapy as a profession. *Journal of Poetry Therapy*, *19*(3), 133–145.

Frank, K. (2000). The management of hunger: Using fiction in writing anthropology. *Qualitative Inquiry*, *6*(4), 474–488.

Gaines, B. (2018). Edutainment tonight: Nightly news as a mix tape. *Textshop Experiments*. Issue 5.

Gerge, A., Wärja, M., & Pedersen, I. N. (2017, Feb.). Using aesthetic response: A poetic inquiry to expand knowing, part I: The Rx6-method. *Voices: A World Forum for Music Therapy*, *17*(1).

Glaw, X., Inder, K., Kable, A., & Hazelton, M. (2017). Visual methodologies in qualitative research: Autophotography and photo elicitation applied to mental health research. *International Journal of Qualitative Methods*, *16*(1), 1609406917748215.

Green, E., & Kloos, B. (2009). Facilitating youth participation in a context of forced migration: A photovoice project in Northern Uganda. *Journal of Refugee Studies, 22*(4), 460–482.

Hanzalik, K. (2019). Creating art in a critical research and writing course. *Double Helix*, 7.

Hanzalik, K., & Odeh, N. with contributions from Mihigo, C., & LoseLose, M. (2021). *"The artist's process" in arts-based research methods in writing studies*. New York: Routledge Books.

Harper, D. (2002). Talking about pictures: A case for photo elicitation. *Visual Studies, 17*(1), 13–26.

Hodges, C., Cutts, W., & Fenge, L. (2012). *Seen but seldom heard: Challenging perceptions of disability*. For Bournmouth University, Fern Barrow, Poole, Dorset, UK.

———. (2014). Challenging perceptions of disability through performance poetry methods: The "Seen but Seldom Heard" project. *Disability & Society, 29*(7), 1090–1103. doi: 10.1080/09687599.2014.907775.

Holm, G. (2015). Participatory photography: Language minority teenagers' sense of belonging? *ETD. Educação Temática Digital, 17*(1), 211–227. https://www.fe.unicamp.br/revistas/ged/etd/article/view/7094.

———. (2020). Photography as a research method. In P. Leavy (Ed.), *The Oxford handbook of qualitative research* (2nd ed.). Oxford, UK: Oxford University Press.

Holm, G., Sahlström, F., & Zilliacus, H. (2018). Arts-based visual research. In P. Leavy (Ed.), *Handbook of arts-based research* (pp. 311–335). New York, NY: Guilford Press.

Immigration and Hate Crime Resources. (n.d.). *We are all immigrants*. New York State Office of the Governor. https://www.ny.gov/programs/we-are-all-immigrants.

Intke-Hernández, M., & Holm, G. (2015). Migrant stay-at-home mothers learning to eat and live the Finnish way. *Nordic Journal of Migration Research, 5*(2), 75–82.

Irwin, R. L., Bickel, B., Triggs, V., Springgay, S., Beer, R., Grauer, K., . . . & Sameshima, P. (2009). The city of Richgate: A/r/tographic cartography as public pedagogy. *International Journal of Art & Design Education, 28*(1), 61–70.

Jones, K. (Director). (2014). *Rufus stone: The movie*. Dorset, England.

Jones, K., & Leavy, P. (2014). A conversation between Kip Jones and Patricia Leavy: Arts-based research, performative social science and working on the margins. *Qualitative Report, 19*(38), 1–7.

Kalmanowitz, D. (2013). On the seam: Fiction as truth: What can art do? *Journal of Applied Arts & Health, 4*(1), 37–47.

Kraehe, A. M., & Brown, K. D. (2011). Awakening teachers' capacities for social justice with/in arts-based inquiries. *Equity & Excellence in Education, 44*(4), 488–511.

Kuttner, P., Sousanis, N., & Weaver-Hightower, M. B. (2017). How to draw comics the scholarly way: Creating comics-based research in the academy. In P. Leavy (Ed.), *Handbook of arts-based research* (pp. 396–423). New York, NY: Guilford Press.

Latif, M. M. A. (2019). Using think-aloud protocols and interviews in investigating writers' composing processes: Combining concurrent and retrospective data. *International Journal of Research & Method in Education, 42*(2), 111–123.

Latz, A. O. (2017). *Photovoice research in education and beyond: A practical guide from theory to exhibition*. New York, NY: Routledge.

Lawrence-Lightfoot, S. (n.d.). *Sara Lawrence-Lightfoot*. Retrieved from Saralawrence lightfoot.com.

Lawrence-Lightfoot, S., & Davis, J. H. (1997). *The art and science of portraiture*. San Francisco, CA: Jossey-Bass.

Leavy, P. (2009). *Method meets art: Arts-based research practice*. New York, NY: Guilford Press.

———. (2012). Fiction and critical perspectives on social research: A research note. *Humanity & Society*, *36*(3), 251–259.

———. (2013). *Fiction as research practice: Short stories, novellas, and novels*. Walnut Creek, CA: Left Coast Press, Inc.

———. (2015). *Low-fat love: Expanded anniversary edition*. Boston, MA: Brill Sense.

———. (2016). *American circumstance: Anniversary edition*. Boston, MA: Brill Sense.

———. (2017). Introduction to arts-based research. In P. Leavy (Ed.), *Handbook of arts-based research* (pp. 3–21). New York, NY: The Guilford Press.

LeBlanc, N. (2018). The abandoned school as an anomalous place of learning: A practice-led approach to doctoral research. In M. Cahnmann-Taylor and R. Siegesmund. *Arts-based research in education* (pp. 174–189). Abingdon, UK: Routledge.

Lenette, C. (2019). *Arts-based methods in refugee research*. Singapore: Springer.

Lenette, C., Brough, M., Schweitzer, R. D., Correa-Velez, I., Murray, K., & Vromans, L. (2019). "Better than a pill": Digital storytelling as a narrative process for refugee women. *Media Practice and Education*, *20*(1), 67–86.

Lightn1 (2017, Jan. 25). In C. Baker, Is Syracuse a sanctuary city? Can Trump pull federal funds? 6 answers about immigration policy. *Syracuse.com*. https://www.syracuse.com/news/2017/01/i.

Marback, R. (2009). Embracing wicked problems: The turn to design in composition studies. *College Composition and Communication*, *61*(2), W397–W419.

Marlowe, J. (2018). *Belonging and transnational refugee settlement: Unsettling the everyday and the extraordinary*. Abingdon, UK: Routledge.

Martiniello, M. (2015). Immigrants, ethnicized minorities and the arts: A relatively neglected research area. *Ethnic and Racial Studies*, *38*(8), 1229–1235.

Marsh, J. S., Dyer, M. J. A., Bubp, R. L., & Myers, J. (2017). Fiction as method in qualitative research. In J. Matthes (Ed.), *The international encyclopedia of communication research methods* (pp. 1–6). Hoboken, NJ: Wiley-Blackwell.

McIntyre, A. (2000). Constructing meaning about violence, school, and community: Participatory action research with urban youth. *The Urban Review, 32*(2), 123–154. https://doi.org/10.1023/A:1005181731698

McNiff, S. (1998). *Art-based research*. Philadelphia, PA: Jessica Kingsley Publishers.

———. (2008). Art-based research. In J. G. Knowles & A. L. Cole (Eds.), *Handbook of the arts in qualitative research: Perspectives, methodologies, examples, and issues* (pp. 29–40). Los Angeles, CA: Sage Publications.

———. (2012). Opportunities and challenges in art-based research. *Journal of Applied Arts & Health*, *3*(1), 5–12.

Morrow, R. A., & Brown, D. D. (1994). *Critical theory and methodology*. Thousand Oaks, CA: Sage Publications.

Nayebzadah, R. (2016). The truth behind fiction-based research. *Journal of Humanistic and Social Studies*, *7*(2), 49–61.

Neilsen, L. (2008). Lyric inquiry. In J. G. Knowles & A. L. Cole (Eds.), *Handbook of the arts in qualitative research: Perspectives, methodologies, examples, and issues* (pp. 93–102). Los Angeles, CA: Sage Publications.

New American Forum (2019). New American Forum panel discussion at Art Rage Gallery. Syracuse, NY.

Norris, J. (2011). Towards the use of the "great wheel" as a model in determining the quality and merit of arts-based projects (research and instruction). *International Journal of Education & the Arts, 12*(1).

Oliviera, E. (2009). MoVE (method: visual: explore): Marginalized migrant populations and the use of visual and narrative methodologies in South Africa. *African Studies Review, 68*(2), 197–214.

O'Neill, M. (2008). Transnational refugees: The transformative role of art? *Forum Qualitative Sozialforschung/Forum: Qualitative Social Research, 9*(2).

———. (2019). Women, art, migration, and diaspora. In B. Dogramaci & B. Mersmann (Eds.), *Handbook of art and global migration: Theories, practices, and challenges* (pp. 132–142). Berlin, Germany: Walter de Gruyter.

Porcelli, L. (2017). A new restaurant run by refugees is revolutionizing one of America's poorest cities. *Saveur*. https://www.saveur.com/with-love-syracuse-refugee-restaurant/.

Prior, P. (2014). Tracing process: How texts come into being. Reprinted in E. Wardle & D. Downs (Eds.), *Writing about writing: A college reader* (2nd ed., pp. 492–524). New York, NY: Bedford St. Martin's.

Rappaport, L. (2013). Trusting the felt sense in art-based research. *Journal of Applied Arts & Health, 4*(1).

Richardson, L. (1994). Nine poems: Marriage and the family. *Journal of Contemporary Ethnography, 23*(1), 3–13.

Rolling, J. H. (2013, 1963). *Arts-based research primer*. New York: Peter Lang Publishing.

Rotas, A. (2004). Is "refugee art" possible? *Third Text, 18*(1), 51–60.

Rubino, V. (2019). The artistry of composition: Design thinking in writing studies. In K. Hanzalik & N. Virgintino (Eds.), *Exquisite corpse: Studio-art based writing in the academy* (pp. 125–148). Anderson, SC: Parlor Press.

Saldaña, J. (2003). Dramatizing data: A primer. *Qualitative Inquiry, 9*(2), 218–236.

———. (2005). *Ethnodrama: An anthology of reality theatre*. Lanham, MD: Rowman Altamira.

———. (2016). *Ethnotheatre: Research from page to stage*. Abingdon, UK: Routledge.

Sanctuary policies: An overview. (2017, Feb.). American Immigration Council, Washington, DC.

Sanders, J. H. (2006). Performing arts-based education research: An epic drama of practice, precursors problems and possibilities. *Studies in Art Education: Arts-Based Research in Art Education, 48*(1), 89–107. doi: 10.1080/00393541.2006.11650501.

Schuler, G., Oliveira, E., & Vearey, J. (Eds.). (2016). MoVE project, Izwi Lethu. African Centre for Migration and Society, University of Witwatersrand, South Africa.

Scott, T. (2009). *Dangerous writing: Understanding and political economy of composition*. Logan, UT: Utah State University Press.

Seabrook, D. (2017, Oct.). Performing wellness: Playing in the spaces between music therapy and music performance improvisation practices. *Voices: A World Forum for Music Therapy, 17*(3).

Shipka, J. (2011). *Toward a composition made whole*. Pittsburgh, PA: University of Pittsburgh Press.

Sigona, N. (2014). The politics of refugee voices: Representations, narratives, and memories. In E. Fiddian-Qasmiyeh, G. Loescher, K. Long, & N. Sigona (Eds.), *The Oxford handbook of refugee and forced migration studies* (1st ed., pp. 369–382). Oxford, UK: Oxford University Press.

Sinner, A. (2013). *Unfolding the unexpectedness of uncertainty: Creative non-fiction and the lives of becoming teachers*. Rotterdam: Sense Publishers. doi: 10.1007/978-94-6209-356-0.

Skinner, J. (2003). Montserrat place and mons'rat neaga: An example of impressionistic autoethnography. *Qualitative Report*, *8*(3), 513.

Smagorinsky, P. (1994). Think-aloud protocol analysis: Beyond the black box. In P. Smagorinsky (Ed.), *Speaking about writing: Reflections on research methodology* (pp. 3–19). Thousand Oaks, CA: Sage Publications.

Sousanis, N. (2018). Thinking in comics: An emerging process. In M. Cahnmann-Taylor & R. Seigesmund (Eds.), *Arts-based research in education* (pp. 190–199). Abingdon, UK: Routledge.

Stoller, P. (1984). Sound in Songhay cultural experience. *American Ethnologist, 11*, 559–570. https://doi.org/10.1525/ae.1984.11.3.02a00090

Sullivan, G. (2010). *Art practice as research: Inquiry in visual arts* (2nd ed.). Thousand Oaks, CA: Sage Publications.

Surman, J., & De Johnette, J. (2002). *Invisible nature*. Germany: ECM Records.

Tomlinson, B. (1984). Talking about the composing process: The limitations of retrospective accounts. *Written Communication*, *1*(4), 429–445.

Tulloch, K. (2018). Somali refugee shares Syracuse resettlement story: "Here, I help myself" (video). *Syracuse.com*. https://www.syracuse.com/living/2018/06/from_somalia_to_syracuse_fadumo_warsame_shares_story_for_world_refugee_day_2018.html.

Ulmer, G. (2019). Konsult scenario: Genre for electorate learning. In K. Hanzalik & N. Virgintino (Eds.), *Exquisite corpse: Studio art-based writing in the academy* (1st ed., pp. 63–86). Anderson, SC: Parlor Press.

Van Maanen, J. (1988). *Tales of the field: On writing ethnography*. London: The University of Chicago Press.

Viega, M. (2016). Science as art: Axiology as a central component in methodology and evaluation of arts-based research (ABR). *Music Therapy Perspectives*, *34*(1), 4–13.

Wang, C., & Burris, M. A. (1997). Photovoice: Concept, methodology, and use for participatory needs assessment. *Health Education & Behavior*, *24*(3), 369–387.

Wood, M., & Brown, S. (2011). Lines of flight: Everyday resistance along England's backbone. *Organization (London, England)*, *18*(4), 517–539. doi: 10.1177/1350508410387961.

Wright, T. (2014). The media and representations of refugees and other forced migrants. In E. Fiddian-Qasmiyeh, G. Loescher, K. Long, & N. Sigona (Eds.), *The Oxford handbook of refugee and forced migration studies* (1st ed., pp. 460–472). Oxford, UK: Oxford University Press.

Zhang, K. (2018). Being pregnant as an international PhD student: A poetic autoethnography. In M. Cahnmann-Taylor & R. Siegesmund (Eds.), *Arts-based research in education: Foundations for practice* (pp. 67–81). Abingdon, UK: Routledge.

3 Representing Research in Art Form

The previous chapter discusses reasons why a researcher might want to take up ABR and some methods they might want to use. I offer a set of genres that researchers might want to use for any stage of the research process, along with some of their strengths and limitations. I describe the methods and purposes for my own project as well. Representing research is a slightly different story. It is easy to assume that a researcher simply needs to select a genre that seems most fitting and then, after some reflection on the genre, data, purpose and audience, conform the data into the genre. However, representing the research in art form is much more complex. What is happening in the process of representing the research is the process of knowledge making, a highly recursive process that Graeme Sullivan (2010) refers to as "transformative research" practice (p. 110). Sullivan is a visual artist-researcher, so he is specifically speaking about visual arts creation, but the theory seems applicable to many contexts. Sullivan contends, knowledge creation is

> Recursive and constantly undergoes change as new experiences "talk back" through the process and progress of making an art in research settings. This transformative feature also applies to the artist-researcher, who is very much an embodied part of the research process as . . . arts knowledge is framed, encountered, created, as insight is revealed and communicated.
>
> (p. 110)

As the researcher engages in this transformative practice of research, they are engaged in three processes, which converge like a braid, the metaphor Sullivan uses (pp. 113–115). The researcher engages in self-reflexivity, where the researcher considers their creative and personal interests as they interpret and bring the data into art form. At the same time, the researcher engages in dialogue with the data. The data shapes the researcher's vision for the text as the researcher shapes the data. This dialogue can be extended out to the audience as well, since after the art form has materialized, the project engages in a dialogue with the audience. As self-reflexivity and dialogue occurs, the researcher questions the way they are representing the research in art form. For example, the researcher might ask, should the color of an image be different? Should more exposition correspond with a scene? In answering these questions, the researcher considers the data, the purpose, the audience, and the context to which the researcher is using the project to respond.

I would argue that this transformative process, particularly when done collaboratively with research participants as co-creators, is an emotional, intellectually rigorous process and product, one that can, although does not have to, demonstrate some degree of technical mastery. I will reflect upon this idea at the end of this chapter, but first, I am including the representation

What Is It like to be home?

It means you can lay on your bed
Stare at the wall
Count the stars
wear your slippers
Hug your pillow
Sleep till noon
closing your eyes
Dreamlike a child
Ride the clouds
Once I had a home
Four walls
One roof
One door
One window in my room
Flowers on my blanket
Painting on the wall
Bookshelves my dad hung for me
With the books I adore

Once I knew what it feels like being at home
Nada Odeh
7/ 12/ 2016

Figure 3.0 Poem by Nada Odeh

of the research, which, as the reader will notice, at a glance is not a short story but rather a mixed-media text that does not adhere to any generic standard or aesthetic formula.

The Artist's Process

In 1981, Mmalanibwa LoseLose's aunt decided to teach her 19-year-old nephew how to make traditional decorative cloth. Ufumatji Wa Mashuka was part of Congolese culture. People placed them on tables, chairs, couches, or beds. "If someone did not have Ufumatji Wa Mashuka, it was like something was missing from that person, so [the artist] would provide that to them." The patterns were limited only by the artist's imagination.

LoseLose was given supplies—a white bedsheet, a pencil, a needle, yarn-like thread, and a ruler. He imagined a colorful geometric pattern that he loved,

> something that I needed to see, something that I loved so much that I wanted to see it materialize in the way I thought of it. Love has no rules, no regulation. If you love something, then you need to see it.

He sketched the pattern that he loved onto the bedsheet using the ruler and pencil, then sitting comfortably, he placed the sheet on his lap and the large ball of thread at his side. He pulled the thread out far past his body, threaded it into the needle and began stitching the pattern in an upward motion. His sinewy arms stretched up and down, back and forth, in rhythmic motion with the thread, sometimes for hours. He did this for many years, and on many occasions the thread would turn into knots. Sometimes, "I would have to demolish it. If something went wrong, I had to tear it apart. If I made a mistake, then I would have to repair the mistakes."

Over time, he became a schoolteacher who taught history, geography, and French. After work, he would come home and sew, inside his house or outside, wherever it was, it did not matter. Once he was finished, he would give it as a gift. Giving was the way of his Evangelical community. People cherished Jesus, solidarity and community, and the everyday practices that sustained them (Marlowe, 2018). In the evenings, neighbors would gather for dinner. They would provide for their neighbors if they were in need. They laughed with genuine smiles. Yet extraordinary political violence soon fractured their world and ultimately changed the fate of millions of Congolese people (Marlowe, 2018).

The Cities of Destruction

By1997, violence in the Democratic Republic of Congo became relentless. Laurent Kabila, leader of the Congolese rebel group, Alliance of Democratic Forces for the Liberation of Congo (ADFL), overthrew president Marshal Mobutu (Turner, 2013). This followed an invasion by the

Rwandan Banyamulenge Tutsis, who invaded refugee camps for Rwandan Hutus in the eastern Congolese cities Uvira, Bakavu, and Goma. As lives were upended, Rwanda attempted to seize Congo by attacking Kabila, and freeing and then training members of Mobutu's army, who had been captured by the AFDL to aid in their cause (Turner 2013). The cause: power? minerals? tribalism? regionalism? religion? The war: Africa's world war? A Civil War? An International War? A Resource War? Complexities seemed to aid and abet voluble interpretations of what was going on in ways that served various stakeholders around the world, affectively suffocating the defenseless reality that millions were massacred as Kabila proclaimed that he and the AFDL were pawns in Rwanda's sick game (Turner, 2013). In the process, a "war against women" raged, with all political players contributing in some way, allegedly including the United Nations (Turner, 2013, p. 120). Women en masse were raped, many were infected with HIV/AIDS, and widowed after their sons and husbands were murdered (Turner, 2013).

LoseLose's world had broken apart. Millions of people, including he and his brother, fled to neighboring Tanzania as if it were some sort of refuge. He was forced into a refugee camp where, as he says, "life was very hard." Instead of living in comfort, he lived in a tent. It was hard to find food to eat. "I went to bed as if I were not going to get up in the morning." Along his journey, he met new people, the crowds of people who lived in the tent with him, those who would give him rations of food. "Six small bowls of food were provided for two weeks," he said, cusping his empty hands. Even though LoseLose encountered many obstacles, he found opportunities. He met new students and continued to teach geography, history, and French. He found love, married his wife, and had six children. He met people who taught him carpentry. "Each time I found that life was becoming unbearably hard, I was able to produce, to make tables and beds." He continued to make Ufumatji Wa Mashuka too. The decorative cloth took on a new meaning. In encampment, dead bodies were covered in white sheets and laid to rest, so Ufumatji Wa Mashuka, with its bright, colorful patterns, was symbolic of the living. LoseLose said,

> If you had white bedsheets, then it meant you're a dead body. White bedsheets are for people who are dead. The people who are alive needed to have colored bedsheets. If they had colored bedsheets it meant that they were still alive.

He realized that he could make Ufumatji Wa Mashuka for survival. He could sell it. In the past, LoseLose gave his designs as gifts, but in the refugee camp, "life was hard so I expected some payment. I had many clients," he said. Haunted by death, they all wanted to buy from him. "When people learned that I was making the decorative cloth, they would send people to buy it." Life was that way for 20 years. He worked to survive. He imagined patterns that he loved and brought them to life for people who eventually died in numbers.

LoseLose would survive and was granted asylum after a process that took nearly two decades, two presidents--Laurent Kabila credited with inciting war, and his son, Joseph, credited with ending it through negotiations and diplomacy--and great concern about the eruption of violence in the future (Turner, 2013; "DRC," 2016). As DRC changed, LoseLose's life was changing and he had his own concerns. He would be starting over at age 49. He did not speak English. Nevertheless, in pursuit of economic opportunities, survival, peace, and a better life, he began his pilgrimage to the United States.

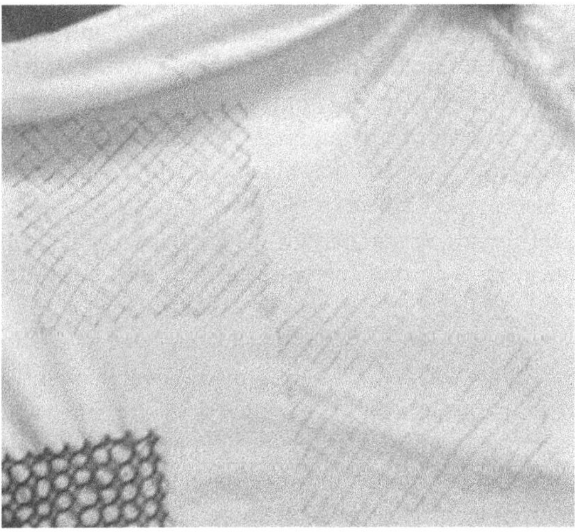

Figure 3.1 Photograph of Ufumatji Wa Mashuka, sketch of what LoseLose said is "something that I needed to see, something that I loved so much that I wanted to see it materialize in the way I thought of it."

Nada Odeh was always known in Damascus, Syria, as the girl who was good at drawing. She began at the age of three. She loved illustrating, using pencils, sketching, and drawing. She also wrote poetry. Art was always her form of expression. "When I wanted to say something, I either create artwork or I write poetry. It's a way of expression, a part of me. I can't separate myself from the art. It's 'we.' We grew up together."

The people in Nada's world made life beautiful. Her mother, Najah Faham, worked for the Ministry of Culture and gave her Arabic translations of colorful Russian storybooks. Reading the books was a visual experience for Nada. She loved the bright colors and the energy they exuded. Najah took Nada everywhere,

> to cultural events, to concerts and art openings that were happening. She always made sure that we were involved because of her work at the Ministry of Culture. So she was very involved in all of the events. . . . Art became not only a tool to express myself but I was also surrounded by art. There were lots of arts activities happening in my life.

Nada's father, Bashir Odeh, taught her the beauty of love and caring.

> He was an educator, a great human, and a loving father and husband. He always supported everyone around him, either family, friends, father, and husband. He raised me and my sister to love everyone around us and care about them. The summers were always fun when my dad took me and my sister to the swimming classes and art classes. He was a pleasant and loving person that planted the love and care seeds in me. He was also a great educator. He was a loved educator and administrator and he always supported his students in their education and communicating with their parents and that was a rare thing back in Syria in the 1980s.

Syria in the 1980s was a time marred by violence within Syria between religious extremist groups and Hafiz al-Assad's regime, which resulted in thousands of civilian lives lost (Lesch, 2019). A black market outpaced an unstable, emerging economy; the government invested all of its capital in military operations to, as it asserted, maintain law and order in a religiously and ethnically diverse Syria and to safeguard itself from the world beyond its borders (Lesch, 2019). Assad the patriarch both designated positions of power for his family members, and offered the Syrian people a mirage where they had some degree of freedom. It was in this climate that Nada was able to bloom as an artist (Lesch, 2019).

She attended the prestigious Adham Ismail art school then earned a fine arts degree at Damascus University. Her work often depicted Arabic houses and Damascus. The lines, shapes, colors, especially gold, were inspired by the Islamic miniatures in the 13th century Arabic book of fables, *Kalīla wa-Dimna*. She went on to teach art at schools in Damascus, Dubai, and the United Arab Emirates. Soon she married and began a family, so art fell to the wayside.

She had no space for herself to make art. She stopped out of fear that the toxic chemicals would hurt her two young children. “It was not realistic to be painting,” she said.

She and her husband eventually separated. He moved to Dubai, and she remained in Damascus and became an outcast.

> To our society, our community, it was kind of a big thing being by myself. People think, “Oh she’s by herself. She’s raising her kids for almost four years.” . . . That means I’m doing what I want to do . . . so the position of being alone and not divorced and having two kids . . . there are lots of conflicts in it. It’s all about gender and power.

As the years passed, scrutiny over Nada’s life continued with and through the patriarchal Syrian government. Al-Assad had died and bequeathed to his son Bashar al-Assad a Syria where the public and private sectors colluded on the black-market for profit, for the ease of exploiting the Syrian people, and for the state’s control (Lesch, 2019; Tarabay, 2018). Under Bashar’s early rule, people were given a semblance of power; some political prisoners were freed, state-controlled media made way for privatized newspapers (Lesch, 2019). Nada, however, wanted equality for women, not the imposition of social roles and gender power plays that permeated her life. She thought of leaving Syria for good. Unable to express herself through her art, she remained silent. She felt “a kind of blockage in [her] soul.” Her world became dark. Where was the beauty that she was knew as a child? The bright colors and characters in the storybooks?

By early 2011, the darkness had become unbearable for Syrians. Arab Spring protests raged throughout the Middle East where people demanded freedom and an end to government corruption (Lesch, 2019). Incited by the movement, Mouawiya Syasneh, a 14-year-old, spray-painted “Your turn, doctor” on a schoolyard wall in the small town of Daraa (Ensor, 2017). Mouawiya was speaking to Bashar, who was an ophthalmologist (Ensor, 2017). No one anticipated the serious impact of what the young artist called “a joke” (Syasneh as cited in Ensor, 2017): torture and imprisonment of the artist and his aristocratic teenage friends; the bruised, beaten, and dismembered body of Hamza Ali Al-Khateeb, shot three times to his death at just 13 years old; protests throughout Syria; airstrikes and chemical attacks in civilian neighborhoods issued by the president; more than 500,000 lives lost, including Mouawiya’s father (Ensor, 2017; Memmott, 2011). Nearly six million Syrian survivors fled to meet a fate as unknown as the fomenting polity in a country ravaged by a history of violence (Lesch, 2019). By March 15, the revolution had begun (Lesch, 2019)

Living in a home that overlooked the presidential palace, Nada watched from her window as men demanded Bashar step down from power. Bodies and weapons figured into Damascus' new landscape. Hundreds of people who could no longer tolerate oppression clashed with military forces alongside the Omaween Fountain near the presidential palace, ornate golden churches, intricately designed mosques, skylines that changed from blues to oranges to red-pinks, emerald rolling hills. Syria was bereft and many starved—the poverty, unusually long drought, and the restriction of access to water had become intolerable (Lesch, 2019). The revolution was a hopeful attempt to create a better future, but it was not without its consequences (Lesch, 2019).

Artists used their art to speak out in protest, but many of them lost their voices. In Hama, north of the capital of Damascus, the famous Syrian revolutionary singer Al Qashoush sang in defiance only later to have his throat cut out by the government (Cooke, 2016). Nada's friend Muhammad, a performance artist and musician, was protesting in Daraa while Nada was at home. "I can still remember that one day he came back voiceless," she said. But she too was voiceless, silenced by Syrian society, the expectations for women, her devotion to her responsibilities as a single mother, and the dangerous political outrage in the streets.

By April, the president acted as if he were conceding (Lesch, 2109). Eventually he continued with his authoritarian ways (Lesch, 2019). Paramilitary groups formed, fractured, and reformed (Lesch, 2019). Many died, many became internally displaced, many fled to bordering countries, such as Turkey or Jordan (Lesch, 2019). Some took dangerous treks by boat to Greece where the risk of travel was less than the risk it was to stay (Lesch, 2019). Nada was hesitant to leave, but she was forced to make a decision. "While we were sitting in [my mother's] house, we saw the snipers on the rooftops. But like, thinking about it, what if the sniper was trying to shoot someone and he shot someone who's not doing anything at all?" More than anything, she needed to protect her children. They fled to California to stay with her brother while her sister and mother, who was then widowed, remained to take care of their responsibilities in Damascus.

Though Nada was no longer in Syria, she did not forget the people who escaped, and the dangerous ways in which they escaped; nor did she forget the role she played, the gossip she endured, the protestors, and the family she had to leave behind. They were her sources of inspiration for the art she was determined to create. Without the violence brought upon Syria by an authoritarian president, and Nada's pure love and devotion to her children that left her no choice but to flee Syria, she would never be the artist she was to become.

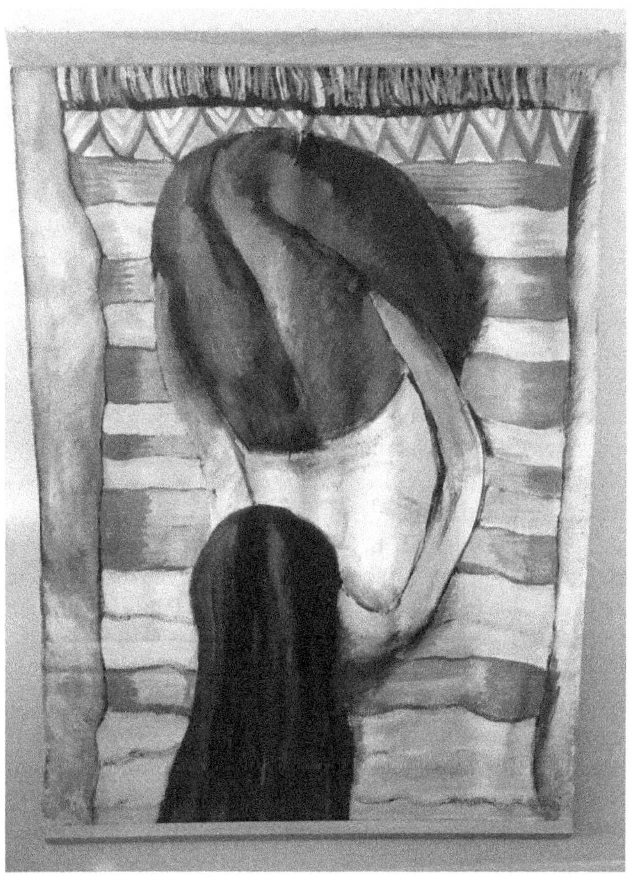

Figure 3.2 Painting by Nada Odeh

(Courtesy of Nada Odeh)

The Sanctuary City

LoseLose arrived in Syracuse, New York, a city of approximately 142,000 people in the middle of Central New York ("Census," 2019). Of all the cities in the nation who take in refugees, Syracuse stands at number 3 (Baker, 2016). The city is a long-time sanctuary for immigrants, and now it is an official Sanctuary City, a place where people can, regardless of citizenship status, have access to employment opportunities, housing, education, and health care without living in fear of deportation, forced separation from their families, and imprisonment (Sanctuary Policies, 2017). In the past ten years, approximately 9,500 former refugees from all over the world have resettled in Syracuse, coming from countries such as Syria, Iraq, Afghanistan, Sudan, Somalia, Bosnia, Burma, Nepal, and the DRC (Allen & Breidenbach, 2017 a, 2017b). The city has been recognized as a place with exemplary resettlement practices, and has a history of welcoming refugees that dates back to 1979 with Vietnamese refugees (OCL, 2012-13). In addition to resettlement agencies, there have been numerous organizations that provide resources for health, housing, language learning, employment opportunities, K12 and college-level education. Innovative, individualized approaches have been taken by some landlords and local businesses to provide new Americans with safe places to live, clothing, furniture, and training to sustain a small business, and learn English (OCL, 2012-13). Some companies have hired refugees regularly and training programs prepare them to work in healthcare, food services, and construction (OCL, 2012-13). Though the process of resettlement, which takes place over the course of nearly five years, ideally culminating in citizenship, is difficult to navigate for both for former refugees and caseworkers (OCL, 2012-13). Local politicians want refugees to live in Syracuse and oppose policies that would keep them from resettling (Miner, 2015; Walsh et al., 2019). Though these factors alone do not make the city a sanctuary, rather it is a complicated social terrain.

Different tribes from the Congolese community have resettled in Syracuse and many brought their tribalism and animosity with them (Mihigo, 2020). For instance, members of one tribe viewed other tribes as lowly (Mihigo, 2020). Members of another had been victimized in Congo by a tribe whose people lived in the same neighborhood in Syracuse (Mihigo, 2020). LoseLose navigated this milieu as he resettled with his wife and children and the values that he learned along his journey: solidarity, support, creativity, his love for Jesus Christ. At the same time, those within the Congolese community became part of an impoverished city characterized by systematic and overt discrimination imposed upon people of color.

Until recently, Syracuse was the ninth most impoverished city in the United States. (Weiner, 2019). Even though the city now ranks eighteenth, nearly half of all children live below the poverty line (Weiner, 2019) and white families earn almost twice as much as families of color (Baker, 2018). However, the media boasts that the economy in Syracuse and the surrounding suburbs was "far outpacing other upstate [New York] cities" (Bolt, 2020). Poverty, or what has been called Syracuse's "crisis of misery" (Eisenstadt, 2016) has impacted the health, education, hope, and wellbeing of Syracuse residents, including former refugees. Most resettle in the most impoverished neighborhood, The North Side, where 40 percent live below the poverty line (Baker, 2016b). Former refugees encounter overt discrimination, as seen in newspaper articles that attempt to teach readers the difference between refugees and parolees (Baker, 2016a) and turn to the economic data to determine if they are a "benefit or burden" (Baker, 2016b). They are met with contempt as seen in the comments section of articles, where refugees become: perpetrators who abuse social services ("we are not an international soup kitchen and welfare state") (Lightin 1 as cited in Allen & Breidenback, 2017), a threat to cultural purity ("No culture or nation can survive if this is not very limited" (Lightin 1 as cited in Allen & Breidenback, 2017), and Others who are not "the Real Citizens of Syracuse in Harms Way" (Chuckyray1 as cited in Baker, 2017).

These epithets echo a narrative perpetuated by former President Trump, who claims that those who live in Sanctuary Cities are "illegal aliens with severe criminal records [resettling in Sanctuary Cities] to terrorize innocent communities" (Trump, 2019). His xenophobia led to an executive order where he set a 45,000-person limit on the number of refugees entering the United States, a limit that is 50 percent less than five years ago, and the lowest since 1980 (Eisenstadt, 2018b). As a result, there are 72 percent fewer new Americans resettling in Syracuse today than in years prior (Breidenbach, 2018). Resettlement agencies are losing funds and caseworkers (Eisenstadt, 2018b). Nevertheless, Trump's claims and can be debunked by cultural, economic, and political realities.

A photography exhibit that honors refugees shows that their experiences in Syracuse cannot be reduced to a single story (Staab, 2019). Chandra, a college-educated woman from Nepal now working every day at a fast-food restaurant, states that "my children are getting a good education" and she describes her house as her "palace" (as cited in Staab, 2019, p. 5); Pramita from Nepal is optimistic since her daughter "will have a childhood I did not have" (as cited in Staab, 2019, p. 9); The American dream of young Mkoma from Somalia is "to make my parents proud" yet she feels that minorities and impoverished people living in Syracuse have fewer chances to make their dreams a reality (as cited in Staab, 2019, p. 10).

In keeping with a national trend, former refugees are becoming politically visible and powerful (Adeola, 2019). In 2019, Chol Majok, a democrat and former refugee from Sudan, won the Third District Common Counselor seat after nearly twenty years of living in Syracuse (Adeola, 2019. Majok was concerned the lack of visibility and agency of former refugees, who did not have a say in policy decisions (as cited in Adeola, 2019). Now Majok's position grants him the power to represent six neighborhoods (Adeola, 2019). His agenda involves ensuring that former refugees have the resources to maintain employment, such as through childcare and transportation (Bior, 2019). Following Majok's election, former refugee Jay Subedi sought a

Common Councilor seat in Syracuse (Adeola, 2019). Former refugees such as Majok often negotiate tensions between opportunity and obstacles, they negotiate a life between two worlds, questioning what cultural traditions and expectations they want to keep and what American cultural traditions and expectations to assume (Majok and Odeh, as cited at New American Forum, 2019).

When LoseLose arrived in Syracuse, he befriended Cyprien Mihigo, who plays many roles for the Congolese community. A former refugee himself, Cyprien is a pastor as well as the founder of the New American Coalition Trust and the Congolese Women's Empowerment Sewing Group. He is someone who will provide transportation for those in need and raise funds for English languag`e lessons and driving classes. Cyprien said, "The divide in society is huge . . . everyone has a different idea. Refugees are contributing to the nation . . . citizens do not share the same perspective with the ideas of the founding fathers . . . awareness has to be there for people to gain understanding" (2019). To accomplish that, he created the play *Cry for Peace: Voices from the Congo*, where Congolese new Americans from different tribes and native Syracuse residents share personal and historical narratives about the Congo that are interspersed with traditional Congolese music (Watkins, 2020). The play, which was developed alongside luminary directors, has been performed in the Congo, in Syracuse, Washington, D.C. and many other locations (Watkins, 2020). The event helped bridge the divide between different tribes living in Syracuse, but not without participants questioning unification, particularly when, for instance, a woman was raped by a member of a tribe in the Congo and then performed in the play with another member of that tribe (Mihigo, 2020). Cyprien's vision of an interconnected and civically engaged community of Congolese new Americans is slowly becoming realized, even if that does not chip away at the conflict inflicted by militia in DRC that ultimately resulted in murders, theft, and the displacement of millions of people between 2017 and 2019 ("DR," 2020; "DR Congo," 2020). He has been happy to see smiles rather than suspicion, and the formation of new friendships (Mihigo, 2020).

LoseLose has enjoyed the support of the Congolese community, but he has also grappled with the cultural, economic, and political challenges of resettlement. He was not fluent in English and needed American credentials to teach. He was ready to make a contribution to the economy, though opportunities were limited.

> For us, the people who age is a little bit advanced, it's difficult to say there is much we can achieve in this country. When the age is advanced,

> and there is a limited time when you cannot work in this country anymore, so the hope according to the age. Hope is not that wide open because I was older when I got here.

But he knew how to survive. "Even though we are old, we have pushed and can survive the system, so there is no other way."

He found a job as a landscaper and continued to make Ufumatji Wa Mashuka. The process was the same, though he did not have access to the thread he wanted, and the way of the world was different.

> Here, [I] have [my] assistance, basic life, basic support. I'm not in that bad of a situation. The hope I have in a refugee camp is different from the hope I have today, and I'm still doing it. Now I own my own house. Here we are doing it because we have been doing it and cannot just give it up. I can do it for yourself or a family member or for someone I know, because I know how to do it. But economically, I don't do it as a business to rely upon to survive. Two different environments, different lives, economies, societies, support.

His craft became a way to relax after work if he wanted. He would watch television and sew. His art was a relief from the struggles he had adapting to American individualism. "Whenever you get into another culture you have to accept the differences. In Africa, people have solidarity. [In the United States], everyone fights for their own life. People are individualists." This impacted how he approached people and what to expect from them, such as "a real smile." Many in the Congolese community maintain a sense of solidarity, which makes a difference, though some do not.

> I can be home and six houses we live in this neighborhood, come home from work, women will bring food for everyone. Visitors bring drinks, beer, have a seat. The whole neighborhood will drink until it is done and they will stay there.

After work, he will work on Ufumatji Wa Mashuka, but there is no pressure to sell it, no need to quickly produce it. It is a symbol of love and reflects the Congolese values for community, solidarity, and tradition. He composes when he wants to for the purpose of giving it to others as a gift. Ufumatji Wa Mashuka has been the thread carrying him through his journey, his means of what was once financial survival and will always be emotional survival, he said. Most recently, he finished one with a vibrant red geometric pattern.

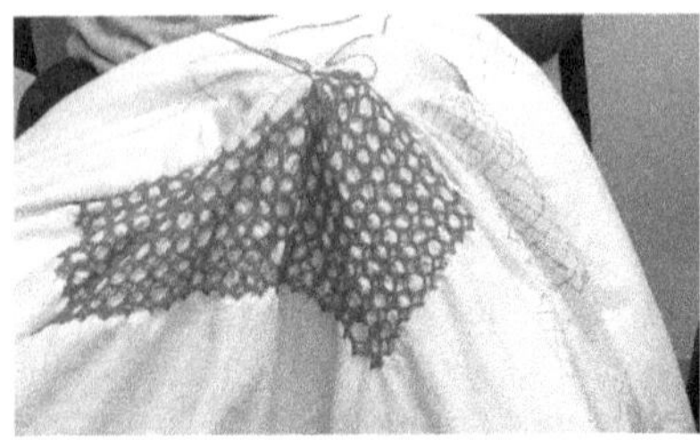

Figure 3.3 Photograph of Ufumatji Wa Mashuka, decorative cloth project

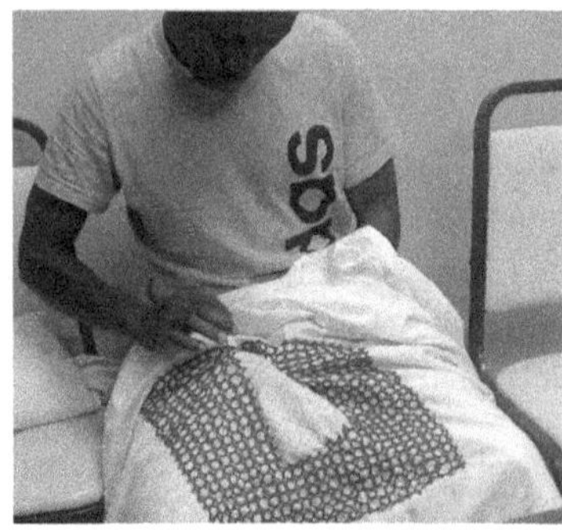

Figure 3.4 Screenshot of Mmalanibwa LoseLose, sewing at St. Stephen's Church, Syracuse

Neverlands

In California, Nada moved in with her brother. She said "I sure I had the space to draw and paint, where I could put I material, where I could create things." Life changed, she learned, she grew, but "I was a guest at someone's house. It was fine but it was kind of very challenging at the beginning trying to understand how this country works and how things function and how to be in this society." She did not need her brother to take care of her, and the price of living in California was too much. She wanted to be on her own.

By 2013, she moved to Ann Arbor, Michigan. She met more people and became more accustomed to some of the everyday practices of American life—the practicalities of renting a house and finding a co-signer and adapting to the weather.

> My first four months were very overwhelming. I think it was my first experience having snow. . . . I was not used to snow, I was not used to wearing all these layers and thick things and boots, so I [began to] understand how to live. . . . But my biggest challenge was not those things. My biggest challenge [was] when I started going out and meeting people. I had this kind of fear, like how can I talk to people? How can we communicate? It [wasn't] the language I was worried about. . . . In Syria, we ask a lot of personal questions. They ask you about your salary, what you are doing. It's very usual. People interfere with everything, versus here, everyone has a line you can't cross if they don't allow you. . . . It's true I spoke English, but I still didn't have the American accent or the American communication way.

Nada found her way by immersing herself in cultural life. While volunteering at an art fair, she learned "things you do not read in books . . . daily living when you are in the Middle East, there's no type of education . . . you have to live [in the United States] to understand." She finally had the perfect studio, too. Her garage.

One day, Nada was volunteering with a group of people from a charity organization. They were putting together care packages of clothes to donate to refugees, but people were donating dirty clothes that were in bad condition. "[I could not] understand the mentality of people thinking that a person who is in a refugee camp can wear trash. How do [people] think [they] can donate this piece for someone to wear it?" She opened a bag and was pleased to find that

> Someone [donated] a whole collection of women's slips and gowns, very nice material, to be sent to refugees in camps. I want to send something in very good condition. I want to send something new not used. . . . One of the women who was helping, and I was kind of surprised, said "What are they going to do with that they are in the camp? Let's take it and we give money instead." I fought for it, and I think she hated me for that.

She came home and started to paint. She used acrylics. "It's fast and simple." Furiously, she began to paint. A portrait of a beautiful girl with long brown hair adorned in a gold crown. A portrait of a beautiful mother wearing makeup and a white veil and an elegant gown, reading to her two children. In both paintings, drab brown tents crowded the backgrounds. She started another painting, this time with a catwalk, the kind celebrities walk down crying for attention when they are exploiting Syrian children. Nada heard her muses, two boys talking to her, trying to speak through her. "I get connected to the characters in my paintings." She painted them. They wore gold crowns and looked out from the catwalk into a faceless crowd at a refugee camp crowded with tents that looked like diamonds. She painted an ornamented celebrity woman desperately clinging to them. The painting was done. She named it "Cat Walk." With those three paintings and nine more, she wanted people to see "refugees' nobility, royalty, and entitlement to sympathy. I believe that refugees in the camps are royalty and they should be treated in the best way. It is not charity. It is solidarity." She named the collection "Royalty in Refugee Camps."

Nada had reclaimed her voice and people listened. She was invited to exhibit her work, starting at Tiffin University in Ohio. Eventually, she led humanitarian workshops in Washington D.C.; Buffalo, New York; and Albany, New York. But she wanted more for herself and for what she could give to the world. She left Michigan for Syracuse to pursue a degree in museum studies at Syracuse University, and her muses followed.

The Sanctuary City

Nada moved to a suburban town in Syracuse, enrolled her children in school, and made a studio in the back of her garage as time marched on in Syria. The question resettlement loomed for millions as the educational system had all but collapsed, with only half of all Syrian children attending school (Lesch, 2019). Homes were destroyed in a military playground where the government and Russia attacked Syrian opposition groups by ground and air (Lesch, 2019). The United States attacked Russia, killing hundreds of people in the Russian military while Israel was at war with Iran, all within Syrian Borders (Lesch, 2019). Beyond Bashar's vision where violence would end in a year and his authoritarian government would be restored, the people questioned if there was an end in sight, and the end they wanted was freedom (Lesch, 2019).

Responding to the violence through her artwork and life in a Sanctuary city, Nada made a name for herself as both a curator and artist: she curated numerous exhibits locally and an entire museum show in Washington, D.C.; she exhibited her paintings at local galleries, created a mural in Arabic calligraphy, led art workshops, and served on a committee for new Americans. She was also thinking about marriage. She found an old wedding dress at an estate sell, bought it for $15, hung on the wall of a museum in such a way as to show a woman hanging like a marionette (Eisenstadt, 2018a). Through the piece, she wanted to ask the questions: "What does it mean for women to have a wedding dress? Does it mean to be locked in a box or does it mean to have more freedom?" (as cited in Eisenstadt, 2018a). She had a voice, and people heard it. But there was a disconnect. She was ready to speak with and alongside, rather than directly at, an audience.

One day, she dressed simply in dark jeans and a zip-up speckled black jacket, then went to her studio to work. She turned on a bright fluorescent light, the kind that mechanics use in garages. Paintbrushes, paint canisters, palettes, and rags covered in paint lay on the ground. Paintings of "Royalty in Refugee Camps" were tilted on the walls in different corners of the room as if they had not seen the light of day. A portrait of her mother, whom she had not seen in many years, lay on an easel on a drawing desk. The piece was called "Muslim Ban."

Her newest work, *We Are Immigrants*, was propped against the center of the wall. She struggled to describe it in words, and sometimes she struggled with painting it, but she had made good progress so far. Four panels depicted a world of interconnected emerald-colored rolling, mostly barren hills, a bright blue sky, and a windy path. Everything was positioned above a wave-like swath of pink-red paint; everything was made with dramatic brushstrokes that lured the viewer's eyes in different directions, and colors that, she hoped, would shift and change the world in the process of revising and collaborating with the local community.

On the far left, there was a panel of Syria: a simple church, the Omaween Fountain that she so loved and remembered vividly, the hills forever in the backdrop of Damascus. The hill seemed to extend to the next panel to a barren place that needed to be brought to life. On the third panel to the right, refugees sailed in a humble rowboat in the middle of the ocean past a large ship en route to Ellis Island. Small details were sprinkled throughout the panels: a little painting of Mount Etna in Sicily, a white cross, a little pink flower, a white boat. These were made by her friends with roots in Vietnam, Thailand, Ireland, and Italy. In her mind, she envisioned more voices added to the piece. How that would look, she had not yet determined.

Today, she wanted to make some progress. She eyed the yellow Syrian church on the far-left panel that would later become blue to match the fountain beside and the sky. She pointed at the church and thought,

> I don't like this yellow; I want to change it. It's very pale. I usually like vibrant colors in my art, strong colors in my art—yellow, red, clean colors, not dirty, and I don't know how to make it nicer. My intention was to make it more golden, but I think I used the wrong yellow because this part is about Syria.

She paused. "And the churches are really nice in Syria. It's not washed down, I feel like this area should be cleaned up a little bit, more color in it." She began to clean it up, adding a more golden yellow.

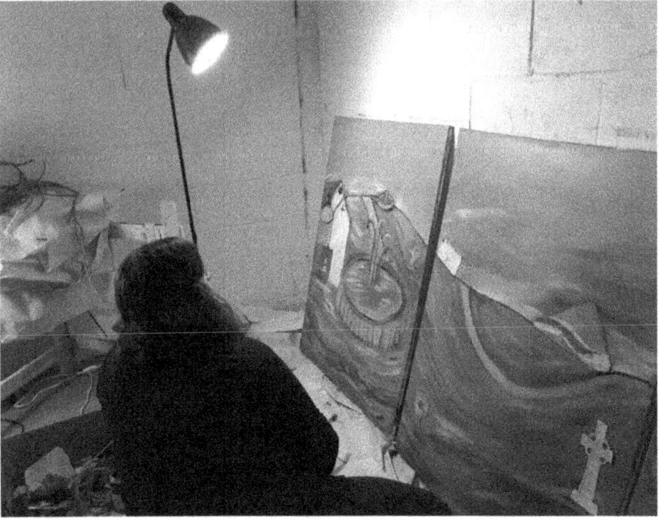

Figure 3.5 Photograph of Nada Odeh, making a yellow Syrian church more golden

Sometime later, she surveyed a row of farmhouses on top of a hill on the far-right panel that would later become a small row of houses. She quietly picked up a paintbrush beside her. She leaned in, added white brushstrokes that lightened the grass. She leaned back, added more paint to the brush. She leaned forward and back with paint again and again, in complete silence, occasionally pausing, turning her head in contemplation. She looked at the painting, all the paintings together, then looked back at the far-right panel. "I want to see how the movement of the brush is working," she thought, gesturing her hand in a wave-like motion. "I want there to be more colors [on the far-right panel], especially the top, so I [need to] start adding color." Sometimes she added yellow and blue and she didn't use the green, but this time, she thought, "I want the green to be mixed on the canvas. I want to see some surprises. . . . I want it to be more spontaneous, not planned. Sometimes, but other parts I want to plan it. It's very, it's just, kind of playing with colors."

She chose the color scheme because she wanted to "bring more energy to the painting." She could have created something dark, but to her, "it is easy to be negative." She said, "I want to be positive." She also wanted to control the viewer's gaze, to "make the eye move from down to top because you always want to start where it is super bright and then go to the other areas." As she painted, she struggled to find order.

> I usually control the subject and the elements in the painting, but in the one here, I can't change a lot. Sometimes [I might not] like [a] shape so I paint over it and start all over again, but here I have specific elements I cannot change. I have to go around it.

She dipped a paintbrush in the bright pink-red paint beside her and began to paint around the edges of the canvases. She needed to be isolated a bit. She needed the paint on the edges "to help me isolate a bit, and [to] unify the [bottom] of the four pieces. It's true there is a line going," she reasoned "but adding this color would resolve the problem of what's going on because it's going to be very strong." She stopped to look. "People will look at it first and then look at everything else more in detail. It's just like adding a frame to it." Hours later, she realized she had lost track of time.

For the next few months, she traveled. She went to a Human Rights Summer Institute in Buffalo, New York. What does being an immigrant mean to you? How are you an immigrant? She wanted to know. She asked dozens of participants to share their answers in art form. A young girl painted the Polish flag on a small canvas and wrote "I am Polish." Nada went to the Gear Factory, a trendy studio space for dozens of artists in Syracuse. She set up her four canvases in front of a large table and instructed participants, "Please get some paper and draw something from your own heritage." They collaged: one contributed a carefully crafted question mark, another drew

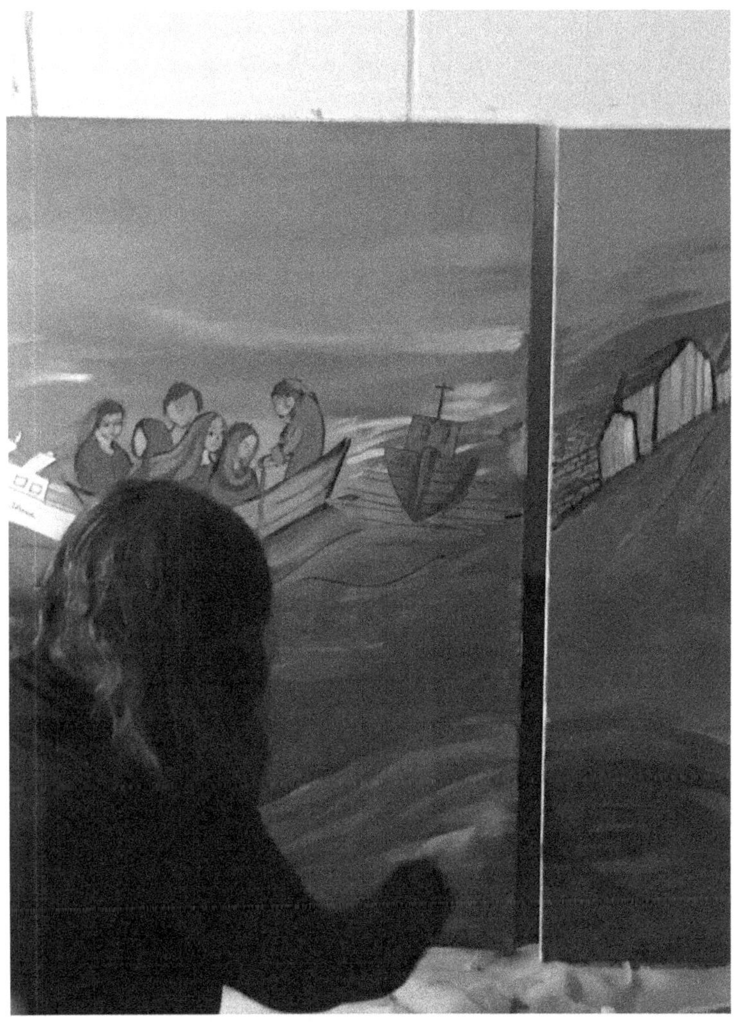

Figure 3.6 Photograph of Nada Odeh, painting her frame for *We Are Immigrants*

the face of Ronald Reagan, and someone else drew a few sheep and a note that said "I am Lithuanian." She went to a small library near her house. She gave a small crowd of people glue, scissors, construction paper, and markers and asked them to create art about their heritage. Someone drew a ship on blue paper. He pressed the drawing in his hand and pushed it far away from him, then looked carefully at it, as if trying to see his place in a broader landscape. Soon enough, Nada amassed dozens of paintings that spoke together.

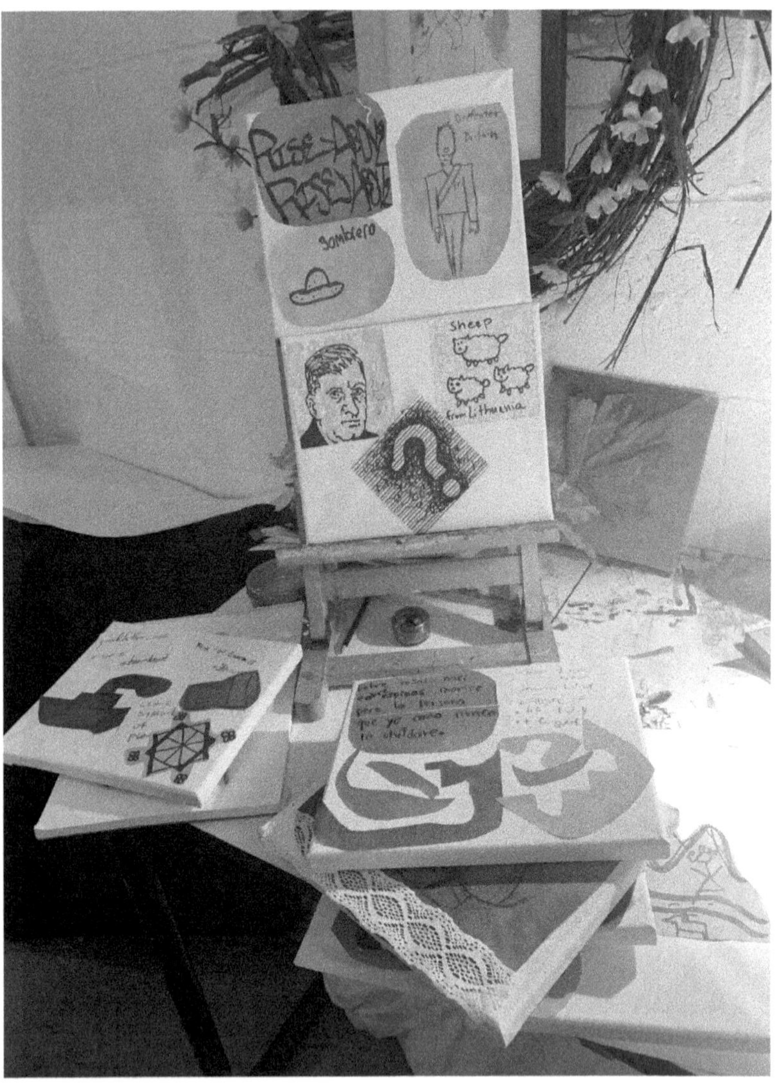

Figure 3.7 Collages from *We Are Immigrants*

A small canvas painted in blue and green presents "Freedom" followed by the Star of David and a menorah. On the periphery was a tree, a pickle, and black branches covered in leaves. Another small canvas celebrated Irish culture and presented the artist's grandfather's migration from Ireland to the United States. It featured a purple steamboat, a note that read "Grandfather

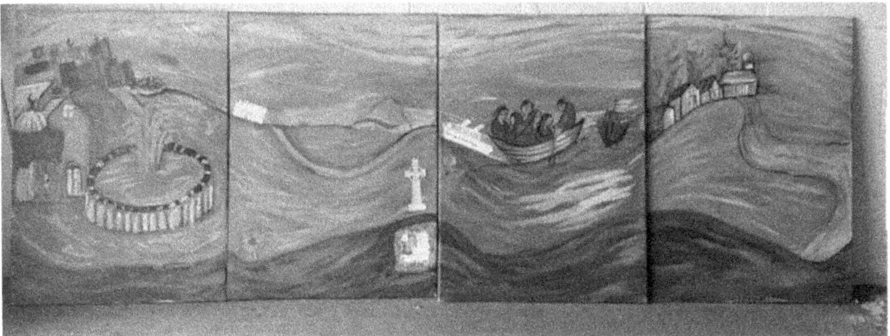

Figure 3.8 The finished version of *We Are Immigrants*

(Courtesy of Nada Odeh)

came on a steamboat," a big glass, a note that read "Pint of Guinness," and a Celtic symbol. A poet contributed a piece as well. The poem read: "The essence of time / as seen before me / looks like it says to hold me / but we can all change / the path, I like / to make my choice / to accept everyone."

Looking at all the work in her studio, she realized what *We Are Immigrants* is all about

> the journey that immigrants go through . . . either by sea or land. The earth's history is built on immigration and travel, and that's how the nations around the world are formed. I wanted to show that we are immigrants in one way or another, even if we are migrating on the same land or another land.

She turned off the bright fluorescent light and went outside in the sun. She was so happy that the air was fresh, that spring was finally there. For the past few months, she looked at the painting and felt like something needed to be added, but it was the first time she looked at it and felt it was almost there.

Creating Sanctuary

New Americans struggle with everyday life and grapple with systemic racism and misperceptions. They want more dialogue and connection, but their art and ties to the community make the sanctuary more of what it can, should, and will be. As Nada said,

> Many new American, refugees and immigrants continue to settle in Central New York and consider it the new home, hoping that they will support other immigrants who come generation later, like Italians and Irish people who helped everyone arrived after them.

Today, Cyprien is re-envisioning the play, *Cry for Peace*. He imagines that the Congolese community could speak about how COVID and Black Lives Matter has impacted them. He is also trying to find a new home for the Congolese Women's Empowerment Sewing Group, a group that one day hopes to host a fashion show.

LoseLose recently learned how to use the sewing machine and now makes dresses. He gave the first two to his wife.

And Nada began a huge mural, "Munjed's Majesty," on a building in a popular neighborhood in downtown Syracuse. Using her signature dramatic brushstrokes of blues, pinks, reds, oranges, and yellows, she painted a Middle Eastern landscape and one of the oldest *souks* (open market) in Damascus. The landscape is accented by an angel that foregrounds the painting. In Arabic calligraphy, she wrote "Salam" (peace). Syracuse is "raging for a change," she said, "and bring[ing] more diversity and eliminat[ing] segregation."

> For more information about Nada Odeh or to find ways to donate, please visit her website at www.nadaodeh.com/contact.
>
> For more information about LoseLose's fabric art, the Congolese Women's Empowerment Sewing Group, and the New American Coalition Trust, please contact Cyprien Mihigo at cyamigo@msn.com. Donations are welcome. Clothes and accessories are available to purchase.

Theoretical Notes

Representing research is a process of knowledge creation. It is transformative and includes self-reflexivity, dialogue, and questioning. This transformative practice, when done collaboratively with research participants as co-creators, is an emotional and intellectually rigorous process and product, one that can, although does not have to, demonstrate some degree of technical mastery.

The experiences of co-creating "The Artist's Process" involved collaborating with the participants and the genres in a way that was highly recursive, open-ended, and often unexpected. Writing the story was an emotional and an intellectual process where meaning changed and developed over time with various art forms over the course of several months, concluding the day before the manuscript was due to the publisher. The impressionistic autoethnography as a short story took many different directions to become what is presented here.

I will explain the aesthetic elements of the composition (e.g., story structure, symbols, character development) in the following chapter, but for this chapter I will briefly speak about the transformative process of representing research. It is important to first mention that a surprising aspect of the process is that a participant dropped out the days before the manuscript was due. When I started the process, I drafted the impressionistic autoethnography as a short story and shared it with the participants, and they made minor changes, such as fact-checking. But as the months progressed, the story changed. Nada's artwork developed; it took different directions—she brought it with her to different events, where more contributors added to the composition. She engaged in dialogue with the audience, which then reshaped her composition, and in turn shaping our composition. Additionally, she decided to change the title of the painting after dialoguing on social media with community members. Her self-reflexivity, along with dialogue and questioning, influenced the direction of our composition. This in turn, resulted in how the data was to be interpreted in art form. The meaning of the painting changed, and I revised some aspects of the story to reflect that change.

My self-reflexivity changed the composition as well. I felt as if I had too much control over the composition—deciding upon the story structure, analyzing the data through the concurrent everyday and extraordinary analytical framework (Marlowe, 2018, p. 36), determining what to include, what to exclude, and how the genre and framework would influence what was said. The participants did recommend changes to the draft I wrote, but I wanted them to have more of a say in ways that were expressive to them. I questioned the formal elements of the composition self-reflexively and happened in dialogue with the research participants as co-creators. I wanted to ensure they adequately expressed themselves in ways that were satisfying to them. However, it was important to keep in mind that sustained conversation was better suited for participants who preferred to be more engaged in the process.

Nada and I spoke regularly. I asked if she would like to include more details, more genres, or any of her poems. Nada shared a poem that she wanted to include and a painting that reflected the poem. Both expressed how she frequently felt, which was homesick. She wanted to add more material about her father as well because he was influential. This in turn re-shaped the composition and where I would add details to the story. At the proposal stage, the publisher recommended that I include images of the artists composing, which factored into the representation of research as well. Thankfully this opportunity was available to us because the visual elements became integral to the story. To be collaborative and co-creative, I asked if the participants wanted to choose the specific photographs from my meetings with them or any other photographs; Nada provided me with additional ones from which to choose. Ultimately, the participants allowed me to choose, so I based my decision on those images that reflected key moments of the composing processes. I took my own photographs and wanted to use some of them. It was a challenge for me to take the right pictures and edit them so they fit in with the narrative. As the shape of the story evolved, the expectations for the genre changed to serve our purposes. This was an exciting, emotional experience but one that required constant negotiating between the goals for the piece, the messages that we wanted to convey, and how they would be arranged.

Engaging in dialogue with Cyprien changed the art form, enriched the everyday/extraordinary theme, and made the process more participatory. At the same time, the context led to some questioning and reconfiguring of the story. The more that was added, the more authentic the piece became, which required careful analysis and intellectual rigor to piece the new meaning together, but this was also why the process was exciting and emotionally gratifying. The more authentic and participatory the piece became, the more it became ethical in the sense that each person contributed to the extent that they wanted and had continual opportunities to contribute. As mentioned, the surprise changed the trajectory of the piece. It also served as an impetus for a shift in perspective from first to third because it brought the artists' stories to life without the distractive first person. In the end, the surprise both enhanced the story and elucidated ABR.

Takeaways

- Representing research in art form is as much a method of data collection and analysis as it is a portrayal of the research.
- Representing research in art form is a transformative process, particularly when done collaboratively with research participants as co-creators; it is an emotional, intellectually rigorous process and product, one that can, although does not have to, demonstrate some degree of technical mastery.
- When co-creating artworks with research participants, it is important to encourage participants to share their ideas and perspectives, if participants are interested and willing. Improvisation is necessary when representing research in art form. Surprises can happen in the process of art making, so researchers should not only be prepared to adapt but also see them as serendipitous opportunities.
- Art forms can be stretched, hybridized, mixed, and innovated as the project develops, if it helps to serve the project's purpose.

References

Allen, P., & Breidenbach, M. (2017a). Refugees in Onondaga County: Where are they from? When did they arrive? *Syracuse.com*. https://www.syracuse.com/news/2017/02/refugees_in_onondaga_county_where_are_they_from_when_did_they_arrive_1.html.

———. (2017b). See the number of Syrian, other refugees resettled in Onondaga County in 2016 (map). *Syracuse.com*. https://www.syracuse.com/data/2017/01/250_syrian_refugees_syracuse_area_2016_obama_trump.html.

Baker, C. (2016a, Mar. 14). Refugees, immigrants, asylees, parolees: What's the difference? *Syracuse.com*. https://www.syracuse.com/poverty/2016/03/refugees_immigrants_asylees_parolees_difference.html.

———. (2016b, March 14). "Refugees in Syracuse: Benefit or burden? Here's what the numbers say." *Syracuse.com*. Retrieved from https://www.syracuse.com/poverty/2016/03/refugees_in_syracuse_benefit_burden.html

———. (2018, May 18). Racial income gap in Onondaga County among worst in the nation. *Syracuse.com*. https://www.syracuse.com/news/2018/05/onondaga_county_has_7th_worst_racial_income_gap_in_us.html

Bolt, C. (2020, January 14). Syracuse region economy growth far outpacing other Upstate cities: 2019 Centerstate CEO Data. *WAER*. Retrieved from https://www.waer.org/post/syracuse-region-economy-growth-far-outpacing-other-upstate-cities-2019-centerstate-ceo-data

Breidenbach, M. (2018, Jan. 23). New refugees drop 72 percent in Syracuse area in Trump's first year: A 10-year low. *Syracuse.com*. https://www.syracuse.com/state/2018/01/refugee_arrivals_drop_72_percent_in_onondaga_county.

Census, US. (2019). *Quick facts*. Syracuse, City, New York. Retrieved from https://www.census.gov/quickfacts/syracusecitynewyork

Cooke, M. (2016). *Dancing in Damascus: Creativity, resilience, and the Syrian revolution*. New York, NY: Routledge.

Chuckyray1 (2017, Jan. 25). In C. Baker, Is Syracuse a sanctuary city? Can Trump pull federal funds? 6 answers about immigration policy. *Syracuse.com*. https://www.syracuse.com/news/2017/01/.

DR Congo Emergency. (2020). *UNHCR: The UN refugee agency*. Retrieved from https://www.unhcr.org/en-us/dr-congo-emergency.html

DR Congo: Thousands Flee Escalating Violence in Kasai Province. (2020). *UNHCR: The UN refugee agency*. Retrieved from https://www.youtube.com/watch?v=Wg66U3eqbm4&feature=emb_title

DRC President Joseph Kabila: Reformer or Corrupt Authoritarian? (2016, October 29). *DW*. Retrieved from https://www.dw.com/en/drc-president-joseph-kabila-reformer-or-corrupt-authoritarian/a-36935441

Eisenstadt, M. (2016, Mar. 10). The cost of poverty: Syracuse's crisis of misery touches all parts of life here. https://www.syracuse.com/news/2016/03/syracuses_high_concentration_of_poverty_touches_all_facets_of_life_in_the_city.html.

——. (2018a, April 16). A Syrian refugee tells the story of Syracuse's welcome: 'A very cozy, homey place." Syracuse.com https://www.syracuse.com/entertainment/erry-2018/04/404d20c0c12562/a_syrian_refugee_tells_the_sto.html

———. (2018b, Aug. 1). Trump policies stop the flow of refugees to Syracuse, once a resettlement magnet. *Syracuse.com*. https://www.syracuse.com/news/2018/08/trump_policies_stop_the_flow_of_refugees_to_syracuse_once_a_resettlement_magnet.html.

Ensor, J. (2017, March 15). Six years of war in Syria: "I regret that so many innocent people had to die," says the boy whose defiance sparked the conflict. *Telegraph.Co.Uk*. Retrieved from https://libezproxy-syr.edu.libezproxy2.syr.edu/

login?url=https://www-proquest-com.libezproxy2.syr.edu/newspapers/six-years-war-syria-i-regret-that-so-many/docview/1877661755/se-2?accountid=14214

Lesch, D. W. (2019). *Syria: A modern history*. Hoboken, NJ: John Wiley & Sons.

Lightn1. (2017, February 9) in Allen, P. & Breidenbach, M. (2017a). Refugees in Onondaga County: Where are they from? When did they arrive? *Syracuse.com*. Retrieved from https://www.syracuse.com/news/2017/02refugees_in_onondaga_county_where_are_they_from_when_did_they_arrive_1.html

LoseLose, M. (2019, Fall). Personal interviews.

Majok, C. (2019, October 9). New American forum panel discussion. *ArtRage*. Syracuse, NY.

Marlowe, J. (2018). *Belonging and transnational refugee settlement: Unsettling the everyday and the extraordinary*. Abingdon: Routledge.

McMahon, J. (2019, Nov. 5). Chol Majok to win Syracuse council seat, becoming 1st refugee to hold office in city. *Syracuse.com*. https://www.syracuse.com/politics/cny/2019/11/chol-majok-to-win-syracuse-council-seat-becoming-1st-refugee-to-hold-office-in-city.html.

Memmott, M. (2011, May 31). In Syria, the death Of 13-year-old Hamza creates a child martyr. *NPR*. Retrieved from https://www.npr.org/sections/thetwo-way/2011/05/31/136812581/in-syria-the-death-of-13-year-old-hamza-creates-a-child-martyr

Mihigo, C. (2019–2020, Fall–Summer). Personal interviews.

Odeh, N. (2019–2020, Fall). Personal interviews.

———. (2019, October 9). New American Forum Panel Discussion. Syracuse, N.Y.

Onondaga Citizens League 2012–2013 study, Report No. 32, The world at our doorstep.

Quick Facts: Syracuse New York (2019, July). *United States Census Bureau*. https://www.census.gov/quickfacts/syracusecitynewyork.

Sanctuary policies: An overview. (2017, Feb.). American Immigration Council, Washington, DC.

Staab, M. R. (2019). Artist statement and Catalogue. Recreating home: Photographs of the refugee experience. Art Rage Gallery.

Sullivan, G. (2010). *Art practice as research: Inquiry in visual arts*, 2nd ed. Thousand Oaks, CA: Sage Publications.

Tarabay, J. (2018, Mar. 15). For many Syrians, the story of the war began with graffiti in Dara'a. *CNN*. https://www.cnn.com/2018/03/15/middleeast/daraa-syria-seven-years-on-intl/index.html#:~:text=Teens'%20graffiti%20ignited%207%20years%20of%20civil%20war&text=In%20his%20neighborhood%20in%20the,inextricably%20linked%20with%20Syria's%20war.

Trump, D. (2019, Sept. 13). *Remarks by President Trump at the 2019 House Republican Conference Member Retreat Dinner. Briefing Statement*. Whitehouse.gov. https://www.whitehouse.gov/briefings-statements/remarks-president-trump-2019-house-republican-conference-member-retreat-dinner-baltimore-md/

Turner, T. (2013). *Congo*. Cambridge, UK: Polity Press.

Watkins, G. (2020, September 22). *The performance that eased a tribal conflict. We are not divided, a reason to be cheerful project*. Retrieved from https://wearenotdivided.reasonstobecheerful.world/congo-cry-for-peace-ping-chong-tribal-conflict/

Weiner, M. (2019, Sept. 26). Census: Syracuse's poverty rate remains among nation's highest. *Syracuse.com*. https://www.syracuse.com/news/2019/09/census-syracuses-poverty-rate-remains-among-nations-highest.html#:~:text=Syracuse's%20poverty%20rate%20tied%20for,edging%20out%20Buffalo%20(30.1%25).

4 Methodological Disclosure in Arts-Based Research

As the previous chapters have shown, ABR involves realizing motivations, determining methods, creating art, and engaging in a transformative process that results in a creative product. This chapter will discuss methodological disclosure, the practice of critical reflection that should happen after the completion of an ABR study, and the ethical implications to which such disclosure lends itself. This chapter provides broad theories that researchers can consider for their projects, and to illustrate, I will reflect on my own ABR project.

Methodological disclosure is crucial for several reasons. First, it is ethical; it divulges the creative liberties that the researcher has taken (Leavy, 2009) and provides a space for the researcher to announce their subjectivity (Lee and Finney, 2005; Lenette, 2019). Methodological disclosure is also useful to other researchers because it reports results and in turn provides greater insight into the strengths, challenges, and processes of a particular project and ABR more broadly (McNiff, 2013; Coemans and Hannes, 2017); it engages the audience of a study (Howard, 2004; Rydzik et al., 2013); it clarifies and enriches the audience's understanding the meaning made through a study, which helps the researcher achieve their purpose (this is especially important if the artistic text is intended to promote social change) (Leavy, 2009). Furthermore, methodological disclosure can enhance the credibility of ABR; more ABR projects and more reflection about them leads to more awareness and acceptance (Leavy, 2009). Yet despite the affordances of the practice, more is needed from arts-based researchers (Coemans and Hannes, 2017).

As the literature suggests, there is no set formula for methodological disclosure, in the sense that researchers can reflect on any number of factors. ABR researchers are encouraged to share the results with the scholarly community, either in a journal article, an edited collection, or at a conference presentation. This would entail describing the research design, reporting the results, reflecting on the research process, discussing the success and challenges, reflecting upon ethical issues, and offering recommendations for future research (Coemans and Hannes, 2017). Coemans and Hannes (2017) also recommend that researchers disclose why they chose one method instead of another, their credentials creating art. Along with Viega (2016), Coemans and Hannes recommend reflecting on how those credentials influenced the artistic approach. Such information would determine if the researcher was "equipped to guide these arts-based research processes" or the question of the researcher's authority to conduct ABR is necessary in the first place. Furthermore, researchers could reflect on their own personal engagement with the project, explaining, for example, "whether its goals have been made, the text of new learning, and personal satisfaction with the overall experience" (McNiff, 1998). Ultimately, addressing any number of these topics would advance knowledge of and practices for ABR.

Scholarly articles about research projects are common, but what makes ABR unique is that methodological disclosure can/should take place in different settings beyond scholarly settings because they are often intended for the general public. For example, if the project culminates in a performance, the researchers can disclose the methods following the performance. This would lead to dialogue, thus enriching the project, affirming its ethical nature, and further achieving its purposes (Leavy, 2009; Viega, 2016). Similarly, if the project results in an art installation, the methods can be disclosed in an artist's statement. A novel or poem might offer an afterword that discloses the methods as well.

In this chapter, I disclose the results of my ABR research project, noting that the methodology was able to answer some of the questions but not all. I reflect on my research process, illustrating how it was ongoing, unpredictable, surprising, and ever-changing—at times limiting, and at times as a success. Furthermore, I reflect on ethics—first, by sharing my subjectivity, next, by disclosing the aesthetic decisions and how they were informed by ethics in relation to a guiding framework/theme and attention to craft, and, finally, by discussing researching with/about marginalized people. Throughout the disclosure, I recommend practices and considerations discovered from my ABR project that researchers might find useful when/if they decide to create their own. Finally, I conclude this section with a note about assessment—the questions, challenges, and implications of reaching audiences and obtaining grants, tenure and promotion, and graduate degrees.

Research Results and Processes

The arts-based data collection strategies answered some research questions, although not without limitations. The project inquired into the ways ABR might enhance process research methods. The project revealed that the think-aloud protocols could not adequately capture the process (TAPs).

Each time I asked a question, the artists stopped to explain the answers, which distorted the process. Moreover, the process of recording the TAPs was distracting. For the sake of accuracy, I took pictures and recorded the demonstrations. The technology—adjusting it, moving it in different directions to zoom in on particular details—was disruptive. Additionally, the artists did not complete their artwork in one session. I was only able to capture a portion of the entire composing process, a process that was already distorted because of the method of documentation. Because of those limitations, the artists' processes could not adequately and accurately be captured. The TAPs occurred in places that were comfortable to them (LoseLose, at his church and the site of the Congolese Women's Empowerment Sewing Group; Nada, at her studio). The location did not prevent the distractions and distortions, however. The TAPs were useful because even though my questions disrupted the composing process, the answers that the artists provided revealed useful information about composing with purpose, making decisions, and problem-solving while also giving them space to express themselves. They also provided crucial visual (gestures, how they composed) and aural (intonations) details about the artists' processes and contexts that could then be translated into art form.

Similarly, the project demonstrated the unpredictability of the retrospective interviews (RIs). The compositions were open-ended, so it was impossible to rely on obtaining the data. Neither Nada nor LoseLose had a set day/time for when their compositions were going to be finished. This was partly because of the nature of their composing processes as informed by their contexts. Nada finished the project eight months after the interview, and I met with her several times before the point at which she had felt the piece was finally finished. LoseLose had no specific plan to finish his artwork, although he finished in two weeks, working on it every day.

The RIs and TAPs were useful because they did provide insight into how the artists evaluate their own work when they are finished (both artists were pleased), and how they problem solve (to collaborate, Nada works around what others have to say while giving the composition a frame that makes everyone's voices cohere; LoseLose starts over). In fact, their ways of trouble shooting—finding ways to harmonize with others and starting over—are themes that play out in their artistic processes and everyday lives. How they grappled with creative blocks (Nada takes breaks and does something completely different, such as going on hikes; she will also reflect on her purpose and why it matters), and strategies for invention—wholly distinct from, if not taboo for, critical writing processes—that embody artistic ways of knowing (Nada listens to the guidance of the characters in her artwork who speak through her; LoseLose imagines a pattern in his mind that he loves and materializes it).

ABR helped confirm the limits of conventional process research methods, but it also enhanced the methods so the process and the methods by which they are documented are understood in new ways. For example, elements to the ethno-mimeses compensated for the limits to the TAPs and RIs by providing a more nuanced view not only of the process but of the role context has on the process and how they are inextricably linked. TAPs do not adequately account for context. Participants typically start the demonstration, think aloud, then finish, and that is the procedure. This assumes that context is irrelevant to how composers think and do their composing, which is limiting. The introductory life-story interview enhanced what could be learned about the role of context in the composing process. The EMs revealed that it is important to consider the broad and complicated context surrounding the composer and their project, particularly since it weighs so heavily on the composer's purpose and composing decisions in the moment. For example, Nada's voice was silenced for many years. When she decided she wanted to create a collaborative composition, she had difficulty negotiating her style with the style of other composers. She had to learn how to work around them while keeping her voice intact, which, she said, was one of the biggest challenges she has faced as an artist. For LoseLose, the past influences where, when, and why he composes today, which in turn also changes the tenor and duration of his composing process. He does not have access to the threads he was used to, but he adapted.

ABR was productive in shedding light on new composing strategies, and the connections between art and writing. The project also showed that ABR is a tool that can convey the everyday and extraordinary experiences of new American artists, and how art mediates both. Through a narrative that wove together character development with the development of war in both the DRC and Syria, and tensions in Syracuse, the attempt was not to show how LoseLose and Nada were victims, but rather how they were forced into dangerous oppressive circumstances that were out of their control. The discussion of how they navigated resettlement showed their heroism and resilience. At the same time, the everyday experiences were discussed—for Nada, it was adapting to American customs such as boundaries for talking about one's life, and what to do living in a place where it snows a lot. For LoseLose, it was finding employment and enjoying life with his neighbors and friends in the Congolese community. Throughout the narrative's trajectory, more light was shed on how Nada and LoseLose's artistic practices evolved throughout the unique processes of resettlement. It also adds to research about the experiences of displaced women. A strong theme in her work, and as such in the narrative, is gender and power. As Nada grew as an artist and woman, her work was shaped by Syrian culture, which she said was all about "gender and power." She responded to this experience in her artwork after she was displaced. The subject matter, productivity, and visibility of her visual art were impacted by motherhood, displacement, and resettlement. Her poetry reflects on her nostalgia, homesickness, and her memories being a daughter.

It is important to acknowledge that I constructed the written narrative based on conversations with the artists, research about the politics, history, and refugee crises in the DRC and Syria. Nada's poetry and paintings, along with images of the artists composing, added to the authenticity in a way that the narrative I constructed could not have. I also added in photographs to the narrative in a way I believed would authentically depict the artists. In chapter 2, I mentioned that Sigona (2014) argued that books that memorialize refugee experiences by bearing witness and preserving memories are important in building strong diasporic communities with "raw material" that comprise that memory that can be passed on to future generations (p. 376). My contribution could be seen as bearing witness; however, the "raw material"—quotes, artwork, pictures of the artists' composing—are more important in preserving those memories that might then be passed on. Moreover, research about resettlement in Syracuse specifically shows that social networking is vital for new Americans' well-being; it is important that new Americans have a platform to share their experiences and stories, while remaining in communication with those who wish to support them, and this project endeavored to accomplish that (Holtz & Mucitelli-Heath, 2012–13).

The ABR project does shed some light on the relationship between public policy, economics, law and new American art, although not in a way that is clear cut. Can art such as Nada's and Cyprien's challenge negative stereotypes that contribute to banning former refugees? This ABR projects cannot answer that question, nor can it show how art making contributed to the artists' upward mobility or the economy at large. While less is known about how Nada's work, for instance, influenced policies, it is apparent that she has left left a mark in Syracuse culture, and beyond, through her artwork, curations, presence at events, and media coverage about her and her work. It is clear how free speech allows for her to share her viewpoints through her art whereas in Syria expressions are often controlled by the state. The ABR project also shows that not all new American artists want to create art that can change public policy and public perception. They simply want to create their art in peace and to share it with those they love; sadly, these artists are the rare exception due to a policy that few asylum-seekers benefit from.

ABR methods during the data collection stage did lead to insights, although they did have their limits. The first pertains to the ethno-mimesis. Typically, an ethno-mimesis involves participants either working with an artist or creating their own artwork (O'Neill, 2008); however, the artists for this study had already started creating their projects before the study took place. It is unclear if the ethno-mimeses provided some measure of healing for the participants; they naturally create art for healing purposes, so the ethno-mimeses would not have contributed to that; it simply provided another opportunity for them to work on an art project that they had already started. Finally, the extent to which the ABR project will contribute to the greater good (e.g., other disciplines, beyond the discipline, public policy, the participants) is unclear. The project will give voice and visibility to the participants through the publication of this book and the circulation of the short story to a broader audience; nevertheless, as McKean (2006) noted, "it would be naive to think that one project alone can radially transform either the individual or the system within which they have to operate" (as cited in Coemans and Hannes, 2017, p. 41). Their point applies to the everyday and extraordinary experiences of former refugees, and it also applies this project's wish to push academic boundaries. The project did not radically transform the expectations for academic writing. As I mentioned in chapter 2, I intended to adapt the creative piece by not using scholarly conventions for formatting and language, such as parenthetical documentation and the use of jargon, in order to connect with a broader audience. This ABR project shows that ABR can stretch the boundaries of academic conventions only so far in certain circumstances. For example, the publisher wanted to incorporate visual art and photograph, which enhanced the piece. They were also very receptive to including poetry. These opportunities had to converge with academic conventions. For example, each image needed to correspond to a figure number, though the captions enhanced the story. Moreover, the parenthetical documentation was a requirement, but the use of jargon was kept to a minimum, particularly by showing the analytical framework in action rather than explaining it. Furthermore, while the in-text citations might be atypical for a general reader, they do not prevent a general reader from accessing the text in the way a more jargon-heavy academic piece would. If the goal is to challenge academic conventions, then ABR can achieve that in ways that are most appropriate for the scholarly outlet or a given situation. I had the opportunity to create an entire book about ABR to share theories and ideas with scholars in the discipline.

The next limitation, although not a problematic one, concerns self-discovery. ABR promises to allow the artist to inquire into their own lives through art form. I was interested in learning about the artists to reflect on my past, but instead, I began to reflect on my present way of life. By listening, observing, and later writing about Nada and LoseLose, I was able to understand an insider perspective about the impact American individualism has on people who value solidarity. Nada and LoseLose live in solidarity and community. LoseLose and Cyprien defined "individualism" as the attitude a person must do for themselves and keep to themselves. As a lifestyle, the Congolese community gets together for dinner every night and reaches out to each other for even the smallest needs (e.g., salt for a meal they are making, a ride to an appointment). The participants were always open to sharing and expressing. LoseLose knows a "real smile" when he sees one. Their encounters, feelings, and perceptions resulted in questions: how much should they reveal? How much should they ask? How much can they rely on someone? How much can they help a stranger? Why is it unusual for neighbors to gather as groups and enjoy dinner together on a regular basis? Their perspectives made me want to shift my priorities. LoseLose does not feel compelled to create artwork according to a set schedule. Nada lives from her heart and produces what speaks to her. They simply go about living their lives, sharing in a community, feeling moved, and expressing that through their art whenever they want. All of that was inspiring to me and made me rethink my way of life. I did not set out trying to learn any of that through this project, but it was the lesson that found me. In other words, ABR can lead to personal insights, but not necessarily in a predetermined way. Researchers might expect to make surprising discoveries about themselves that they did not intend for in the first place.

Aesthetic Decisions as Ethical Decisions in Arts-Based Research

In Chapter 3, I described the process of creating an artistic text, noting the ethical considerations and how my research project took shape collaboratively and independently. The approach toward collaboration was an aesthetic decision rooted in ethics. In conjunction with that, the aesthetic decisions pertaining to craft were informed by ethics that served to accomplish some of the goals for the research project (e.g., providing voice and visibility, providing emic or insider narratives that might be useful to scholars in immigration and the arts and refugee and forced migration studies).

In creating art from data, I was influenced by Jay Marlowe's (2018) argument that while extraordinary stories about former refugees' traumatic experiences are elucidating, they are also Othering and perpetuate stereotypes that assume former refugees are different, powerless victims. Marlowe (2018) contends that everyday stories (e.g., stories about making friends, raising a family, celebrating cultural traditions, creating art) are important in establishing affinities and affirming that people from refugee backgrounds are not individuals who have endured trauma but dynamic and eclectic people who are capable of responding to trauma; everyday stories and extraordinary stories coalesce and enrich each other in such a way as to cultivate more positive resettlement experiences. This perspective is the basis of Marlowe's "concurrent everyday and extraordinary analysis" (2018, p. 36) and the basis of the aesthetic decisions in creating

> The Artist's Process. That is, the aesthetic decisions I made (story structure, scenes, symbols, characterization, and narrative perspective) were rooted in the wish to bring to life the everyday and extraordinary stories in a way that challenges stereotypes and gives people voice and visibility. Moreover, since ABR is an opportunity for a researcher to inquire into their own lives, I wanted to include my own voice in the everyday/extraordinary world of the research participants.

To accomplish that through art form, the initial idea was to take up the impressionistic autoethnography as a short story. The genre is described as "figurative, personalized, fleeting, dramatic, and part realist/confessional" (Van Maanen, 1988, as cited in Skinner, 2003, p. 514). Because I wanted to make the artistic piece accessible to the general public, I adapted the impressionistic autoethnography to become a short story free from jargon and parenthetical citations. However, as the composing process developed, it became apparent that the genre was limiting. The text needed to be multimodal. Moreover, the first-person perspective distracted from and reduced the everyday/extraordinary stories of the artists. Revising the structure was an ethical decision as well as one that enhanced the story.

It is important to emphasize that full disclosure of aesthetic choices is imperative (Leavy, 2009; Viega, 2016). I drew some inspiration from the allegory *Pilgrim's Progress* (1899) by John Bunyan, which was told from the perspective of an omniscient narrator. The protagonist, Christian, lived in the violent "City of Destruction," then took a pilgrimage to the heavenly "Celestial City." Throughout the pilgrimage, Christian stopped in fantasy-like worlds, such as the "Shadow of Death" and the "Delectable Mountains," where he met people, lived, learned, changed, and grew. Eventually, he made it to the Celestial City to revel in its beauty and peace. Bunyan's story is about salvation and that getting to salvation (i.e., the Celestial City) is not easy, and even upon arrival, people are subject to scrutiny. The story structure seemed fitting for the artists' trajectory and better facilitated the everyday/extraordinary framework than the impressionistic autoethnography as a short story.

The story begins with the everyday: LoseLose's aunt teaching him how to create art; Nada as a child learning her art form; egregious violence escalated in both the DRC and Syria, which in turn changed an everyday world (with violence always looming in the backdrop) into two cities of destruction. Scenes, characterization, quotes, and narration about violence and everyday life ensue as the artists make their way from encampment (LoseLose) and the fantastical "Neverlands" of California and Michigan (Nada) to the Sanctuary City of Syracuse, New York. Meanwhile, LoseLose and Nada meet important characters along the way who have changed their perspectives and worlds; for example, LoseLose's wife or a person Nada met in Michigan, whose caustic attitudes toward refugees motivated Nada to create a reactionary collection of renowned artwork. The Sanctuary City presented in "The Artist's Process" is not equivalent to the Celestial City. The scenes, symbols, characterization, dialogue, and narration were intended to reveal that the legal and figurative "Sanctuary City" is not really a sanctuary, but rather a place where the characters grapple with and survive obstacles (adapting to American customs) and the imposition of stereotypes. The story functions then as an interrogation of the meaning of a Sanctuary City in the first place.

Like Christian, the characters left the trauma of the City of Destruction. Unlike Christian, whose pilgrimage ends in a just and heavenly place, the protagonists of "The Artist's Process" did not end up in a sanctuary but, rather, a place with segregation, poverty, and xenophobia, among other challenges. The protagonists in "The Artist's Process" struggled to resettle. LoseLose could not go back to being a teacher, and because of his age, his options for employment were limited. The Congolese community, in particular, endures stereotypes and struggles with language barriers and miscommunication with outsiders. While Nada's experiences in Syracuse have been positive in many ways, her art is partly informed by experiences with xenophobia.

Symbols were used to represent the data in a more artistic way. LoseLose's art form, Ufumatji Wa Mashuka, was symbolic of love and survival; Nada's art forms, painting and poetry, were symbolic of her voice. The motif that held the story together was the entendre of the artist's process since the artists' processes meant both the process of resettlement and the process of art making. Kossak (2018) encouraged arts-based researchers to ask a critical question as they make aesthetic decisions: "Does the aural, poetic, and visual language presented help to enlighten, explain, communicate and expand the overall knowledge base of what is being studied?" (p. 72). As it relates to my project, once the structure changed, the story was better situated to enlighten the readers about the artists' everyday and extraordinary experiences, to offer clear direct, emic narratives or insider perspectives of refugee experiences and resettlement, which provides a more intimate understanding of what people go through, what artists in particular go through, while at the same time correcting dangerous stereotypes.

Some surprises, limitations, and creative liberties pertinent to the story to consider include:

1. Perspective. I intentionally wrote myself into the story to try to reconcile the nostalgia of my past, but I realized that doing so distracted from and reduced the artists' stories. It was too forced. I was also not tied down to the theme of reconciling my past, and I was concerned that I was overdramatizing that part of my life in the first place. Furthermore, I write from a position of privilege, which leads to questions about the right to express the worldview of someone else who has endured trauma and marginalized experiences to which I cannot relate. Additionally, a participant decided to drop out of the study days before the manuscript was due, which changed the narrative and some of the research findings, although that resulted in the emergence of new themes and understandings that were insightful. Finally, Viega (2016) noted that, as an ethical practice, an ABR researcher should acknowledge their creative competencies by articulating an "understanding and positioning [of] one's creative and aesthetic sensibilities and understanding how the dimensions of their craft impact the research process" (p. 34). I have practical and educational experience with creative nonfiction and fiction, but I am not an expert, nor do I claim that the literary techniques used in this composition are par excellence.
2. Structure. Narrative styles from Indigenous and non-Western worldviews could have presented alternate meanings.
3. Creative liberty. Some scenes are true to life but not actually real: the scene in which LoseLose's aunt teaches him his craft; the scene in Nada's studio where she is thinking to herself. The latter scene is derived from my observations of and conversations with her as she composed; the former scene is derived from LoseLose's ethno-mimesis.
4. Characterization and motivation. Fictional characters are better understood in dialogue with other characters (Theriault, 2009). The story could have been enhanced with more dialogue. The data collection tools for my ABR project shed light on some specific scenes from the participants' pasts, although not that many. A different approach to data collection, such as the family photograph technique that prompts the participant to speak about a memory based on a photograph, could lead to more dialogue, more characterization, and a more nuanced portrayal of the research participant. Furthermore, the EM did not lead to details about why or how LoseLose was granted asylum. So, in terms of craft, the story is not propelled forward with motivations and scenarios that

cause domino effects. Nevertheless, what was said by the participants is what they wanted to say, so the story should be left at that.

5. Photography. Taking pictures and editing them took careful consideration, particularly because I am not a professional photographer. I chose them to reflect specific scenes and symbols in the narrative and moments in the composing process. For example, the picture where Nada is painting a red-pink border on two different canvases reflects how that technique helped her "isolate a bit, and [to] unify the [bottom] of the four pieces." By painting the border, she was literally and metaphorically able to isolate from other artists who were composing the composition, yet at the same time, she bridged a divide between them.

The Ethics of ABR Research With/About Marginalized and Vulnerable People

As previously mentioned, it is important to acknowledge issues of ethics during methodological reflection. In fact, methodological reflection is itself an ethical practice not only because doing so will enhance the credibility of ABR, it will also enrich the meaning of ABR projects and provide researchers with experiences that might influence how they design their own projects, which will ultimately lead to best practices. WS researchers have always been committed to ethical research, and they are increasingly drawn to community-based research in new spaces, shedding light on marginalized perspectives in new ways. Looking at examples of ABR projects that pertain to WS might help WS scholars determine how/if they would (co)research marginalized and vulnerable people.

Many scholars are drawn to ABR because it can be participatory (Bradley et al., 2004; Daniels, 2003; Lenette, 2019). Yet with participatory research comes ethical responsibilities. My project demonstrated, when researching with/about former refugees with arts-based methods, it is essential that researchers protect vulnerability and ensure reciprocity while also showcasing participants' agency.

The definition of "vulnerable," according to the Presidential Commission for the Study of Bioethical Issues, is as follows:

> In the context of human subjects research individuals or groups are vulnerable if they are unable to fully and independently protect their one interests, either due to intrinsic characteristics (age or immaturity), or circumstances (e.g. illness, incarcerations, poverty). It is a central tenet of the ethics of human subjects research that additional steps be taken to protect vulnerable participants from harm.
>
> (Vulnerable Population Guidelines, 2016, p. 2)

Additional steps are crucial to protect participants. As mentioned, a participant dropped out of the project days before the manuscript was due. It is important to honor that request without question or pressure. Similarly, it was important to cautiously approach sensitive topics during the ethno-mimeses. Providing the research questions to the participants in advance, continually affirming that they do not have to answer any questions that they do not want to, and encouraging them to take the conversation in their own direction was important. In speaking about their experiences as refugees, I asked, "How have your art practices changed throughout your life given the context of the places you have lived and the experiences you have endured?" This approach was important because it is possible for questions to cause the participant to relive the trauma (Lenette, 2019). With that in mind, Lenette (2019) noted that ethics review boards "position people from refugee and asylum seeker backgrounds as vulnerable, passive 'objects' of research" (p. 91). Her point is similar to Marlowe (2018), who argued that people from refugee backgrounds may have endured trauma, but it is erroneous to assume they are helpless. To that end, I approached the project with sensitivity and asked questions in ways that would showcase the expertise and strengths of the artists.

Reciprocity was essential to my ABR project. This was approached in two ways: "the delivery of direct, tangible benefits to those who participate" (Pittaway and Bartolomei, 2010, as cited in Lenette, 2019, p. 89) and space for the artists to co-create meaning. Regarding the former, I used grant funding to compensate the participants for their time, labor, and materials; wrote and obtained a grant for participants; facilitated networking with participants and Syracuse University, which resulted in a volunteer opportunity and possibilities for future collaborations; provided support with professional writing documents; and provided ways for readers of this book to connect with and support the artists and proposed a university-sponsored event where the artists could speak about and showcase their work to scholars, students, and a non-academic audience. Beyond providing tangible benefits, an important way to ensure reciprocity is through the co-creation of meaning (Lenette, 2019). In regards to my ABR project, it was important to co-create meaning without burdening participants. As an ethic, it is important to acknowledge that ABR is not a panacea, particularly with community-based projects that involve marginalized and vulnerable people (Harding and Gabriel, 2004; Sloane and Wallin, 2013). The benefits of ABR should not be overstated to research participants (Lenette, 2019).

WS researchers might find my experiences useful in approaching their own ABR projects. For example, if a researcher intends to do community-based research with/about marginalized and vulnerable people, it is important to ensure reciprocity (tangible benefits and co-creation of meaning), showcasing participants' agency while remaining sensible to the participants and vigilant to the reasons why ethics review boards consider participants vulnerable. At the same time, it is important to note that ABR projects can be enjoyable and exciting for the participants. In the case of my project, the artists would not create art in the first place if it were not important to them.

A Note About Assessment

Was my ABR project successful? Is the knowledge made through ABR valuable? This is a complicated question considering ABR standards are different from quantitative and qualitative research (reliability, validity, generalizability, etc.) and from context to context.

WS researchers should review the literature about issues of assessment and criteria for evaluation of ABR projects (see Barone and Eisner, 2012; Lafrenière and Cox, 2013; Leavy, 2009, 2017; Leggo, 2008; Norris, 2011; Nelson, 2013; Piirto, 2002). An exhaustive account of that discussion cannot be done in this concise primer. However, particularly insightful perspectives include Kossak (2013), who describes a good ABR project as the ability to "deepen and broaden understanding, comprehension, and overall knowledge of the subject being studied in ways more traditional methods of research cannot," thus addressing the challenge that ABR must "have both the language of the art(s) and scholarly academic speak equally, each as clearly and concisely as possible" and in the end "explain what the research question is attempting to answer" (p. 63). However, Leggo (2008), who said, ask not if ABR is good but rather "What is arts-based research good for?" (as cited in Sinner et al., 2006). In that sense, It is up to the audience to decide if the piece "inspires [them] to reflection, rewards [their] attention with introspection, and moves [them] to ethical, political action necessary to initiate positive change in [their] social interactions" (Finley, 2014, p. 531). Barone and Eisner (2012) offer an important perspective as well. They enumerate six criteria to keep in mind when creating and/or assessing ABR: incisiveness (gets at the central problem without extraneous information); concision (uses concise language so as not to dilute the message); coherence (the parts connect to make a whole elucidating, evocative text); generativity (teaches the reader something new about the world); social significance (the topic matters); and evocation and illumination (an emotional awakening to a phenomenon). Perhaps the most salient point is that criteria can be subject to change, and they should be seen as a way to begin to think about assessing ABR projects (Barone and Eisner, 2012; Leavy, 2009).

The complicated question of how to assess ABR projects has implications for obtaining grants, tenure and promotion, and degree conferral. This is especially important for WS as it struggles to maintain its disciplinary status.

Coemans and Hannes (2017) note that obtaining grants for projects in the social sciences can be challenging because ABR methodologies can be open-ended. As it relates to my ABR project, however, I was able to obtain a grant through the Maxwell School of Citizenship at Syracuse University and its Program for the Advancement of Research on Conflict and Collaboration (PARCC). I was able to obtain the grant because my project was interdisciplinary and could serve disciplines and communities outside WS and the university. My scenario speaks to Franklin's point that artists "bring personal and cultural messages from the edges back to a mainstream center for our collective benefit. It follows then that skillful artistic inquiry is an important form of social research" (2013, p. 91). To that end, when determining research problems or topics, WS scholars should articulate how ABR projects are skillful inquires that might support both WS as well as communities, disciplines, and individuals outside the discipline.

In regard to tenure and promotion, Franklin (2013) notes that the academy wants "tangible accomplishments . . . that yield few results" (p. 91). He recommends that "For ABR to gain acceptance within the academy, we have to absorb the critic's lens and become better at articulating our methods . . . [researchers cannot] avoid adept descriptions of our methodology, processes, and products" (p. 91). Nelson (2013) notes that an analogue to ABR, practice as research (PaR), is viewed with skepticism and that academic capitalism impedes the progress of PaR projects. Loveless (2019) notes that the emergence of research creation (RC), a concept that Leavy (2017) might say belongs under the broader oeuvre of ABR, is an opportunity to challenge the way business as usual is done. She sees RC as a "mode of resistance to individualist, careerist, and bibliometric university cultures." How this resistance might win over tenure and promotion committees has yet to be determined. This complex and relatively uncharted terrain presents an opportunity for WS scholars to engage in dialogue about how, given the particularities of the discipline, ABR and artistic ways of knowing are valuable and can be valuated.

Regarding degree conferral, Sinner et al. (2006) traced a history of ABR dissertations and analyzed 30 across different disciplines, concluding "a commitment to aesthetic and educational practices, inquiry-laden processes, searching for meaning, and interpreting for understanding" (p. 1223). Nelson imagines that a suitable doctoral PaR project is "50/50—the thesis constitutes a substantial [art] practice together with 30,000 to 40,000 words" (2013, p. 11), explaining that this includes a "post-showing conversation" (p. 108) where the researcher engages an audience in a brief dialogue that furthers the purpose of the project (beyond degree conferral) as well as a "viva voice examination" or traditional defense, with, for example, "the replaying of audio or visual material" of the artistic component (p. 110). Furthermore, the doctoral project must clearly show that "the research inquiry . . . is evident in the practice" (p. 112), although the technique does not have to be perfect. This should be reassuring to WS scholars who might not have knowledge on an art form a student takes up. In assessing student projects, Moon (2013) demonstrates to WS that emotional reactions to a text are pertinent when evaluating student work. She notes that "I am not content to rely solely on my analytical mind. . . . I want to feel the burning passion of the researcher and be moved by their intelligent compassionate and creative inquiry" (p. 37). These are just some of the possible considerations that WS should take into account when assessing student work for the purpose of degree conferral.

Conclusion

In this chapter, I have discussed methodological disclosure, which is to say, disclosing one's research methods and critically reflecting on them. There is an inadequate amount of reflection about ABR methodologies, which is limiting. Methodological disclosure is important because it divulges the creative liberties the researcher has taken, and it is useful in that it reports results and in turn provides greater insights into the strengths, challenges, and processes of unique ABR projects, and ABR more broadly, thus enhancing the understanding and credibility of ABR. Depending on the situation, researchers should disclose their methods in both scholarly and public venues. Scholarly articles could explain the research design, report the results, reflect on the process, discuss the success and challenges, and reflect upon any ethical issues, such as aesthetic decisions and researching with/about marginalized and/or vulnerable participants. In a public venue, methodological disclosure could take the form of a dialogue with an audience after a performance, for example. To those ends, assessing ABR projects can be complicated. Some scholars offer criteria that are at once starting points and subject to change. Unresolved complications with assessment can impact degree conferral, tenure, promotion, and obtaining research grants, although these issues might be resolved with more methodological disclosure.

Takeaways

- Arts-based researchers should disclose their research methods to a scholarly audience and, when applicable, to a general audience.
- Methodological disclosure is important because it divulges creative liberties; enriches the audience's understanding of an ABR project; advances knowledge about ABR practices, strengths, and limitations more broadly; and in turn contributes to the credibility of ABR.
- Some scholars offer criteria for high-quality ABR projects, although the criteria should be viewed as evolving and subject to change.

- Complications with assessment of ABR projects can impact tenure, promotion, obtaining grants, and degree conferral; though with more methodological disclosure, these issues can be better addressed.

References

Barone, T., & Eisner, E. W. (2012). *Arts based research*. Los Angeles: Sage Publications.

Bradley, B. S., Deighton, J., & Selby, J. (2004). The "voices" project: Capacity-building in community development for youth at risk. *Journal of Health Psychology*, *9*(2), 197–212.

Bunyan, J. (1899, 2003). *Pilgrim's progress*. Oxford, UK: Oxford University Press.

Coemans, S., & Hannes, K. (2017). Researchers under the spell of the arts: Two decades of using arts-based methods in community-based inquiry with vulnerable populations. *Educational Research Review*, *22*, 34–49.

Daniels, D. (2003). Learning about community leadership: Fusing methodology and pedagogy to learn about the lives of settlement women. *Adult Education Quarterly*, *53*(3), 189–206.

Finley, S. (2014). An introduction to critical arts-based research: Demonstrating methodologies and practices of a radical ethical aesthetic. *Cultural Studies, Critical Methodologies*, *14*(6), 531–532.

Franklin, M. A. (2013). Know thyself: Awakening self-referential awareness through arts-based research. In S. McNiff (Ed.), *Art as research: Opportunities and challenges* (pp. 85–94). Bristol, UK: Intellect Books.

Harding, J., & Gabriel, J. (2004). Communities in the making: Pedagogic explorations using oral history. *International Studies in Sociology of Education*, *14*(3), 185–202.

Howard, L. A. (2004). Speaking theatre/doing pedagogy: Re-visiting theatre of the oppressed. *Communication Education*, *53*(3), 217–233.

Kossak, M. (2013). Art-based enquiry: It is what we do! In S. McNiff (Ed.), *Art as research: Opportunities and challenges* (pp. 19–28). Bristol, UK: Intellect Ltd.

———. (2018). A different way of knowing: Assessment and feedback in art-based research. In R. Prior (Ed.), *Using art as research in learning and teaching* (pp. 61–74). Bristol, UK: Intellect Books.

Lafrenière, D., & Cox, S. M. (2013). "If you can call it a poem": Toward a framework for the assessment of arts-based works. *Qualitative Research*, *13*(3), 318–336.

Leavy, P. (2009). *Method meets art: Arts-based research practice*. New York, NY: Guilford Press.

———. (2017). *Handbook of arts-based research*. New York, NY: Guilford Press.

Lee, J. A., & Finney, S. D. (2005). Using popular theatre for engaging racialized minority girls in exploring questions of identity and belonging. *Child & Youth Services*, *26*(2), 95–118.

Leggo, C. (2008). The ecology of personal and professional experience: A poet's view. In M. Cahnmann-Taylor & R. Siegesmund (Eds.), *Arts-based research in education: Foundations for practice* (pp. 89–97). New York: Routledge.

Lenette, C. (2019). *Arts-based methods in refugee research*. Singapore: Springer.

Loveless, N. (2019). *How to make art at the end of the world: A manifesto for research-creation*. Durham, NC: Duke University Press.

Marlowe, J. (2018). *Belonging and transnational refugee settlement: Unsettling the everyday and the extraordinary*. Abingdon, UK: Routledge.

McKean, A. (2006). Playing for time in "the doll's house": Issues of community and collaboration in the devising of theatre in a women's prison. *Research in Drama Education, 11*, 313–327.

McNiff, S. (2013). *Art as research: Opportunities and challenges*. Bristol, UK: Intellect Ltd.

Moon, B. (2013). Mentoring and other challenges in art-based enquiry: You will figure it out. In S. McNiff (Ed.), *Art as research: Opportunities and challenges* (pp. 29–36). Bristol, UK: Intellect Ltd.

Nelson, R. (2013). *Practice as research in the arts: Principles, protocols, pedagogies, resistances*. New York, NY: Palgrave-Macmillan.

Norris, J. (2011). Towards the use of the "great wheel" as a model in determining the quality and merit of arts-based projects (research and instruction). *International Journal of Education & the Arts, 12*(1).

O'Neill, M. (2008, May). Transnational refugees: The transformative role of art? *Forum Qualitative Sozialforschung/Forum: Qualitative Social Research, 9*(2).

Piirto, J. (2002). The question of quality and qualifications: Writing inferior poems as qualitative research. *International Journal of Qualitative Studies in Education, 15*(4), 431–445.

Pittaway, E., & Bartolomei, L. (2010). "Stop stealing our stories": The ethics of research with vulnerable groups. *Journal of Human Rights Practice, 2*(2), 229–251.

Rydzik, A., Pritchard, A., Morgan, N., & Sedgley, D. (2013). The potential of arts-based transformative research. *Annals of Tourism Research, 40*, 283–305.

Sigona, N. (2014). The politics of refugee voices: Representations, narratives, and memories. In E. Fiddian-Qasmiyeh, G. Loescher, K. Long, & N. Sigona (Eds.), *The Oxford handbook of refugee and forced migration studies* (pp. 369–382). Oxford: Oxford University Press.

Sinner, A., Leggo, C., Irwin, R. L., Gouzouasis, P., & Grauer, K. (2006). Arts-based educational research dissertations: Reviewing the practices of new scholars. *Canadian Journal of Education, 29*(4), 1223.

Skinner, J. (2003). Montserrat place and mons'rat neaga: An example of impressionistic autoethnography. *Qualitative Report, 8*(3), 513.

Sloane, J. A., & Wallin, D. (2013). Theatre of the commons: A theatrical inquiry into the democratic engagement of former refugee families in Canadian public high school communities. *Educational Research, 55*(4), 454–472.

Van Maanen, J. (1988). *Tales of the field: On writing ethnography*. London: The University of Chicago Press.

Theriault, S. A. (2009). Anton Chekhov and the development of the modern character. *Inquiries Journal/Student Pulse, 1*(11).

Viega, M. (2016). Science as art: Axiology as a central component in methodology and evaluation of arts-based research (ABR). *Music Therapy Perspectives, 34*(1), 4–13.

Vulnerable Population Guidelines. (2016). *Presidential commission for the study of bioethical issues*. https://bioethicsarchive.georgetown.edu/pcsbi/sites/default/files/3%20Vulnerable%20Populations%20Background%209.30.16.pdf.

5 A Promising Future for Arts-Based Research Methods in Writing Studies

ABR is an innovative supplement to traditional, empirical, and hermeneutical approaches to research. Artistic ways of knowing can stir emotions, encourage empathy and self-inquiry, promote openness to ambiguity, and encourage people to act, all of which are important for WS at a time when learning, teaching, social justice, and individual well-being are all at stake.

WS researchers continue to find culturally sensitive, transparent, and ethical approaches to inquiry and seek to cultivate new research practices, such as ethnography, narratives, and historical research. They aspire to create opportunities for collaborative research, and research reflection, to make scholarship more public and more personalized. With the recent call for mixed-method approaches to research and new scholarship advocating for approaches to research and pedagogy that embrace ambiguity, failure, transdisciplinarity, and the arts, ABR is a timely and important addition to the production of new knowledge in WS.

As previous chapters have shown, ABR opens the possibility for new purposes for research and new ways to inquire into topics, questions, and problems. ABR approaches are generally flexible, recursive, and open-ended, embracing a diverse assortment of methods, approaches, and genres. Although it can be systematic, there is no single "standard operating procedure" for ABR, and it frequently disrupts conventional research standards (Barone and Eisner, 1997; McNiff, 2008; Leavy, 2009; Sullivan, 2005, 2010). While these qualities can make ABR an attractive option at a time when our discipline is seeking new ways of thinking about the relationship between writing, WS, and systemic injustices, advocates of ABR do not argue that it is suitable for every research question.

A researcher might consider ABR as a means to articulate a research problem or question to shed light on the textures of social reality within, beyond, and among writers and writing communities. ABR creates opportunities to cross disciplinary boundaries by allowing the researcher to experiment with different art forms from sculpture, music, and playwriting to murals, novels, and dance performances. An entire project need not be arts-based. Researchers can pick and choose from a variety of methods. They can collect data through image elicitation and photovoice. They can generate data through collaboratively constructing a play. They can analyze data by attending to intonations, inflections, and gestures. A methodology might change the researcher's motive or incite several additional motives, resulting in a revision to the methodology, a process that might then serve as data for an ongoing ABR methodology.

Possibilities for ABR research designs are endless, evolving, and exciting, although a researcher should not expect a purely entertaining experience. Those seeking to do ABR should be aware that the process is self-reflexive, dialogic, and questioning, which can create uncertainty but can also ultimately produce a transformative experience. Whether carried out independently or collaboratively, ABR is an emotional and intellectually rigorous process. What is perhaps most exciting about ABR for WS is the possibility it offers for shaping new ways of knowing and, concomitantly, new ways of communicating what we know.

Despite its benefits, adopting ABR in any academic discipline, including WS, is not without its challenges. ABR is subject to scrutiny because it does not conform to scientific standards, such as validity and reliability (Barone and Eisner, 2012; Leavy, 2009, 2017), researchers using ABR are not always meticulous in theorizing their work and/or disclosing their methods (McNiff, 1998, 2013; Coemans and Hannes, 2017), ABR can be difficult to assess (Barone and Eisner, 2012), and its findings can often be intensely personal rather than useful to academic and public communities (McNiff, 1998).

Moreover, as WS researchers increasingly draw inspiration from ABR, and as disciplinary appreciation for artistic ways of knowing increases, scholarly outlets will have to adapt. Journals will need to provide for the inclusion of images and other types of media that can capture performances, documentary films, visual art, and more. Journals such as *Textshop Experiments*, *Computers and Composition Online*, and *Kairos* are promising venues for ABR projects, but even these multi-media-friendly journals may need to reconfigure expectations for academic register so that dialogue can take place with a non-academic audience. Furthermore, if ABR is to advance in WS, conference venues will also need to provide spaces and technologies for the presentation of and engagement with artistic texts.

Pedagogical Possibilities

With a growing interest in artistic ways of knowing in WS, arts-based pedagogies are emerging. For example, Daniel (2019) describes an assignment that asks students to attend a performance and take note of the ways bodies impact and interact with stage design, each other, the audience, and other rhetorical factors to convey meaning. This assignment is intended to show students that "writing is composing through bodies" (p. 209). Dredger et al. (2019) discuss a community-engaged project bridging videogame play, fantastical narrative writing, and opera performance as "a way for multiple generations in one community to show the intersections of composition, music, computing, educating, entertaining, and connecting" (p. 104). Brian Gaines's students in an introductory writing course created a video resulting from interviews that they recorded with inmates and law enforcement officials in order to research the prison industrial complex. Gaines noted that for both data collection and representation, "the medium [of video] added a depth to the composition that probably could not have been accomplished within the parameters of a traditional composition assignment" (personal communication, 2020). Based on her compelling research studying the practices of musicians, dancers, and actors and pedagogical practice, Nathalie Virgintino has found that improvisation encourages students to innovate, embrace failure, and take risks while also disrupting academic writing practices that are complicit in perpetuating inequality (2017; Hanzalik and Virgintino, 2019). Vittoria Rubino describes ways to bring a "design disposition" into the composition classroom (2019a, 2019b); Derek Owens (2019) recommends studio-style empathic critique workshops, where students comment on the way a composition makes them feel and the formal elements that cause that reaction; and Megan Nolan teaches a poetry assignment where students use the art form to reconstruct their fractured identities (2019). These are just some of the many wonderful ideas that WS scholars have developed for the teaching of writing. Art is a teaching tool in other disciplines as well. To improve their clinical observation skills, pre-clerk medical students were tasked with describing pieces in an art gallery; study results showed that they improved their skills and that they were engaged in the experience (Lynch and Saks, 2016). Art has also been used to help medical students to identify and reduce their implicit biases (Rubin and Saks, 2020). Moreover, Donna Gustafson, curator for Rutgers University's Zimerilli art gallery, frequently works with students across the disciplines. She argues that examining art enhances critical thinking, cultivates empathy, serves as a catalyst for understanding culture and history, and promotes ambiguity while enhancing argument skills since art is interpretive (2020). The skills Gustafson pointed out are evident in my assignments, where students study works of art at the university art gallery while also enhancing their skills with analyzing visual rhetoric.

In WS, teachers whose work is informed by the Framework for Success in Post-Secondary Writing will be interested to learn that the visual arts and writing share similar pedagogical goals. Writing teachers are encouraged to cultivate a classroom where students gain "habits of mind," such as "curiosity, openness, engagement, creativity, persistence, responsibility, flexibility, and metacognition" (Council of Writing Program Administrators, National Council of Teachers of English, & National Writing Project, 2011). Similarly, in visual arts, educators are encouraged to cultivate "studio habits of mind" by encouraging students to "develop craft, engage and persist, envision, observe, reflect, stretch and explore, understand [the] art world" (Hetland et al., 2007, p. 6). In the visual arts, engaging and persisting requires "learning to embrace problems of relevance within the art world and/or of personal importance, to develop focus and other mental states conducive to working and preserving at art tasks" (p. 6). It also involves "stretching and exploring," which means "learning to reach beyond one's capacities, to explore playfully without a preconceived plan, and to embrace the opportunity to learn from mistakes and accidents" (p. 6). These habits of mind are parallel to the framework's emphasis on persistence, "the ability to sustain interest and attention to short and long-term projects," flexibility, "the ability to adapt to situations, expectations, or demands," and curiosity, "the desire to know more about the world" (p. 1). According to Hetland et al. (2007), reflection in the visual arts is metacognition that involves "learning to think and talk with others about an aspect of one's work or working process" and "learning to judge one's own work and working process, and the work of others in relation to the standards of the field" (p. 6). Visual arts reflection parallels the framework's emphasis on "the ability to reflect on one's own thinking as well as on the individual and cultural processes used to structure knowledge" (p. 1). By carrying out arts-based projects in writing classrooms, students can achieve important habits of mind that can transfer to learning across the disciplines.

It is important to note that just as ABR creates challenges for the evaluation of scholarly work, arts-based pedagogies create challenges for the assessment of student work. Nevertheless, the pedagogical challenges are already quite familiar in WS, and writing pedagogy already provides many options for addressing them. For example, students creating an ABR project might be asked to evaluate their own work, making the case for its usefulness, credibility, and vigor. Moreover, Barone and Eisner's (1997) seven features of literary texts and/or Barone and Eisner's (2012) six criteria for assessment also serve as important standards for quality ABR.

One concern about ABR in the writing classroom is that teachers cannot expect to have mastery over artistic genres. The logic is that, without such mastery, it is impossible to evaluate a student's work (Hanzalik, 2019). This apparent challenge merely creates new writing opportunities, as students might be asked to write a concise reflective paper that explains the methodology used in an art-based project or to write an artist's statement that explains the work of art, the process of composing, the standards for artistic merit, and the extent to which the student believes they achieved technical competence. Jody Shipka (2011), for example, describes asking students to write a statement of goals and choices that explains the types of texts the students are composing within, their goals and choices, and the outcomes.

Conclusion

This book is a primer for using ABR in WS, and I hope it will also serve as a catalyst for continued conversation and invention. While the book recapitulates literature, examples of methods, and practices for reflection, it is impossible to offer a complete picture of ABR. I offer my own experiences with ABR as one example. Throughout the chapters, I discuss, perform, and reflect on an ABR project, drawing connections between the theories I present and my own experiences engaging in ABR. I hope WS researchers will find inspiration here for their own projects. ABR is in its nascency in WS, but the field of WS has a long history of creativity and commitment to learning, teaching, communication, and social justice as well as innumerable talented teachers, researchers, writers, and students. It is my sincere hope that this book will resonate with the WS community and contribute to our recognition of art as a valuable way of knowing and credible means of creating knowledge.

References

Barone, T., & Eisner, E. (1997). Arts-based educational research. In *Complementary methods for research in education* (Vol. 2, pp. 75–116).

———. (2012). *Arts based research.* Los Angeles: Sage Publications.

Coemans, S., & Hannes, K. (2017). Researchers under the spell of the arts: Two decades of using arts-based methods in community-based inquiry with vulnerable populations. *Educational Research Review*, *22*, 34–49.

Council of Writing Program Administrators, National Council of Teachers of English, & National Writing Project. (2011). *Framework for success in postsecondary writing.* Council of Writing Program Administrators, National Council of Teachers of English, & National Writing Project. files.eric.ed.gov/fulltext/ED516360.pdf.

Daniel, M. E. (2019). Dancing = Composing = Writing: Writing about performing and visual arts through dance. In S. Corbett, J. LeMesurier, T. Decker, & B. Cooper (Eds.), *Writing in and about the performing and visual arts* (pp. 201–211). Boulder, CO: University Press of Colorado Press.

Dredger, K., Wyatt, A., Cowden, T., Bukvic, I. I., & Parkes, K. (2019). *OPERAcraft: Intersections of creative narrative, music, and video games.* In S. Corbett, J. LeMesurier, T. Decker, & B. Cooper (Eds.), *Writing in and about the performing and visual arts* (pp. 93–107). Boulder, CO: University Press of Colorado Press.

Gustafson, D. (2020). *Using art for transformative teaching workshop*. Syracuse University Art Museum. Syracuse, NY.

Hanzalik, K. (2019). Creating art in a critical research and writing course. *Double Helix, 7*.

Hanzalik, K., & Virgintino, N. (2019). Social justice in (and beyond) the studio art-based classroom: Improvisation and play as responses to economic inequality. In K. Hanzalik & N. Virgintino (Eds.), *Exquisite corpse: Studio art-based writing in the academy* (pp. 173–196). Anderson, SC: Parlor Press.

Hetland, L., & Teachers College (New York, NY) (2007). *Studio thinking: The real benefits of visual arts education*. New York: Teachers College Press.

Leavy, P. (2009). *Method meets art: Arts-based research practice*. New York, NY: Guilford Press.

——— (Ed.). (2017). *Handbook of arts-based research*. New York, NY: Guilford Press.

Lynch, K. A., & Saks, N. S. (2016). Training and evaluating clinical observation skills in pre-clerkship medical students. *Medical Science Educator*, *26*(4), 539–542. doi: 10.1007/s40670-016-0303-2.

McNiff, S. (1998). *Art-based research*. Philadelphia, PA: Jessica Kingsley Publishers.

———. (2008). Art-based research. In J. G. Knowles & A. L. Cole (Eds.), *Handbook of the arts in qualitative research: Perspectives, methodologies, examples, and issues* (pp. 29–40). Los Angeles, CA: Sage Publications.

———. (2013). *Art as research: Opportunities and challenges*. Bristol, UK: Intellect Ltd.

Nolan, M. (2019). Multiplicity and the student writer. In K. Hanzalik & N. Virgintino (Eds.), *Exquisite corpse: Studio art-based writing in the academy* (pp. 222–243). Anderson, SC: Parlor Press.

Owens, D. (2019). Workshops, critics, and the arts of response. In K. Hanzalik & N. Virgintino (Eds.), *Exquisite corpse: Studio art-based writing in the academy* (pp. 197–221). Anderson, SC: Parlor Press.

Ruben, M., & Saks, N. S. (2020). Addressing implicit bias in first-year medical students: A longitudinal, multidisciplinary training program. *Medical Science Educator*. doi: 10.1007/s40670-020-01047-3.

Rubino, V. (2019a). *The artistry of composition: Towards an arts-based pedagogy for first-year composition*. A dissertation for St. John's University, New York.

———. (2019b). The artistry of composition: Design thinking in writing studies. In K. Hanzalik & N. Virgintino (Eds.), *Exquisite corpse: Studio art-based writing in the academy* (pp. 125–148). Anderson, SC: Parlor Press.

Shipka, J. (2011). *Toward a composition made whole*. Pittsburgh, PA: University of Pittsburgh Press.

Sullivan, G. (2005). *Art practice as research: Inquiry in visual arts*. Thousand Oaks, CA: Sage Publications.

——— (Ed.). (2010). *Art practice as research: Inquiry in visual arts*. Thousand Oaks, CA: Sage Publications.

Virgintino, N. (2017). *Improvisation and studio-based pedagogies in writing studies*. A dissertation for St. John's University, New York.

Index

Note: Page numbers in *italics* indicate a figure and page numbers in **bold** indicate a table on the corresponding page.

For Product Safety Concerns and Information please contact our EU representative GPSR@taylorandfrancis.com
Taylor & Francis Verlag GmbH, Kaufingerstraße 24, 80331 München, Germany

www.ingramcontent.com/pod-product-compliance
Lightning Source LLC
LaVergne TN
LVHW012334100826
845148LV00017B/2284